Negotiations in English

Sanders M. Schroevers, Ian R. Lewis

HAUFE.

Contents

Vorwort

Unsere Welt wird kleiner und geschäftliche Kontakte beschränken sich immer weniger auf den heimischen Markt. Deshalb ist die Kompetenz gefragt, Verhandlungen auf Englisch führen zu können. Effektives Verhandeln, basiert auf zwei Dingen: Verhandlungs- und Sprachkompetenz einerseits, interkultureller Kompetenz andererseits. Denn nur wer versteht, warum und wie der kulturelle Hintergrund den Stil und die Strategie von Verhandlungspartnern beeinflussen, wird international Erfolg haben. Der letzte Faktor ist nicht zu unterschätzen: Eine europäische Studie hat gezeigt, dass rund 40 % der Verhandlungen innerhalb Europas aufgrund von interkulturellen Konflikten scheiterten.

Deshalb gibt Ihnen dieser TaschenGuide zum einen die sprachlichen Bausteine einer erfolgreichen Verhandlungsführung an die Hand. Zum anderen zeigt er Ihnen, wie Sie die entscheidenden kulturellen Unterschiede bei Ihrer persönlichen Verhandlungsführung berücksichtigen. So unterstützt Sie das Buch dabei, Vertrauen aufzubauen und gewinnbringende Vereinbarungen zu treffen – in vielfältigen Interaktionen und Situationen, von der Preisverhandlung bis zum Small Talk. Der TaschenGuide wird so zum ständigen, wertvollen Begleiter bei Ihren Verhandlungen auf Englisch. Wir wünschen Ihnen viel Erfolg dabei!

Sander Schroevers, Ian Lewis

Negotiating skills

This chapter explores a variety of contexts for negotiations, and gives you practical examples of appropriate negotiating behaviour.

Particular attention is drawn to the following negotiation skills:

- Preparation and planning (page 6),
- Socialising and small talk (page 24),
- Understanding different phases of negotiations (page 26),
- Asking questions (page 54) and listening (page 60).

Preparation and planning

In the first century, Cicero, the Roman philosopher and lawyer, wrote: "Ex praeparato, nil desperandum" - preparation reduces trouble. And his adage is still relevant today, because the more thoroughly a negotiation is prepared beforehand, the more likely it is possible to anticipate trouble that might influence a successful outcome.

Experienced negotiators prepare by setting realistic objectives, and thinking about flexible scenarios toward different solutions. We used the word scenario because a negotiation is never a script, where the parties always know exactly what to say and when.

- **Script**: one fixed conversation line
- **Scenario**: an imagined, projected or suggested sequence of events

A scenario will be based around particular key items. Try to be as specific as possible, because unfortunately general objectives tend to render general results. Writing in English in advance will help you to prepare even better. The checklist below may prove a useful tool for developing your ideas for a scenario.

Checklist: preparation

- **Reason**: why are we negotiating?
- **Issues**: which (more detailed) issues will be involved?
- **Settlement objectives**: what do we want, what do they want, what don't we want, and what's our least acceptable result? What is a good alternative to the deal?
- **Priority of issues**: value each issue (high, medium, low importance) and do this for both parties.
- **People**: who is on our team and who is on their team, and what authority do members have? Do all members know their role as part of the team? Do we need a native speaker in our team?
- **Information**: what information do we have? What questions should we ask? What questions will they ask? How should we answer? Which information should be kept? What do we need to verify beforehand? Is there need for calculations, figures or any support materials? Who prepares statistical data and visuals?
- **Offer(s)**: what are our entry and exit offers, what could be theirs and what concessions should we have available?
- **Tactics**: who says what to whom? Who will take notes? Who will listen and observe? What if it doesn't work?

It can be helpful to brainstorm by yourself or with different team members using this checklist. Also realise that despite the fact a team is well prepared, unexpected issues may come up during a negotiation. Sometimes it is necessary to be flexible, or even make alterations to the prepared plans in order to reach an agreement.

> Anticipate 75% of the other party's questions, and prepare suitable answers, preferably already in English.

The above checklist can also help you to evaluate after the negotiation. For instance, to measure to what extent you were prepared for different factors? Or by afterwards measuring how well you anticipated their questions. In so-called negotiation debriefs or reviews, people evaluate what happened during a negotiation. Bear in mind that the objective of such a negotiation debrief is learning, not problem fixing or blaming others. The results of a debrief can be documented for future use, by the same team or by a wider audience. In the words of lawyer and NBA chairman David Stern: "The secret of effective negotiation is dealing from strength, and strength comes from preparation."

Useful vocabulary

call a meeting: eine Sitzung einberufen
attend a meeting: an einer Sitzung teilnehmen
hold a meeting: eine Sitzung abhalten
schedule a meeting: eine Sitzung einberufen
attendee/participant: Teilnehmer
alteration: Änderung
objective: Ziel
debrief: Rückschau

BATNA: Best Alternative To a Negotiated Agreement

The BATNA strategy was introduced by the authors Fisher and Ury in their book "Getting to Yes". BATNA is an acronym for "Best Alternative To a Negotiated Agreement". It is a common tactic used in the English-speaking world. The central idea of this strategy is to think in advance about having alternative options available in order to leave the negotiation comfortably. This empowers you with the confidence to either reach a mutually satisfactory agreement, or walk away to an alternative supplier/buyer or keep things as they are. BATNA comes from planning, brainstorming and preparation with the key players in your organisation. It is a twofold process, as you first need to determine what alternatives are available, and secondly, you need to realistically estimate your counterpart's alternatives. Having a strong alternative strengthens your negotiating powers during the negotiation. If this is weak or you have no alternative, then you feel pressured to close a deal.

Example: BATNA

Horst's company asks him to move to Hamburg; he now earns 70.000 €. He thinks about his alternatives: if he rejects the offer it might influence his position, resulting in a lower paid job within the company, therefore his BATNA is the salary of 60.000 €. He informs on the job market and discovers that he could realistically earn between 80.000 € and 65.000 €; therefore his BATNA is estimated at 75.000 €. By identifying another alternative, Horst has increased his BATNA from 60.000 € to 75.000 €, and thus his bargaining power. Horst also has to estimate the costs of moving to Hamburg, which he believes to be around 5000 €. His BATNA has grown to 80.000 €. Finally Horst will need to realistically estimate his company's alternatives or BATNA. If they have an alternative of moving Horst at a lower price than 80.000 €, a deal will not be easily made. But if Horst believes his skills and his direct usability for the company are to its advantage, he has increased his bargaining power by a total of 10.000 €. For Horst it was not only critical to calculate his own BATNA, but also to make an estimate of the other's BATNA.

The example shows us that both parties have their BATNA. Negotiating is the task of arriving at a reasonable outcome, given each party's next best alternatives. Negotiating is about trying to divide up the surplus, but in such a way that each party benefits. This demands preparation and correct judgement.

Checklist: BATNA

- Brainstorm about your best alternatives if you cannot make this particular deal.
- Elaborate on the most promising alternatives. The best alternative is your BATNA.
- Compare your own BATNA to all offers and proposals.
- When an offer is better than your BATNA, you are in a position to negotiate an agreement.
- When an offer is worse than your BATNA, try to improve on the offer from the other party.
- If the other party does not (or cannot) improve its offer, opt for your BATNA.

Parameters

Parameters are vital for your negotiations. What are the highest/lowest, best/worst, maximum/minimum requirements that are acceptable? These are often referred to as the ideal and fall back (bottom line). Using these parameters wisely helps to clarify what other information is relevant.

- The maximum: lay down what is the very best you hope to achieve. If you aim for a point that remains in a range that is believably possible, you allow yourself the potential of achieving it, having more room for concessions, and giving a stronger chance of reaching a satisfactory outcome. This is often referred to as the ideal.
- The minimum: the acceptable minimum gives you warning signs, when this is being breached and allows you ways to manoeuvre away from this point. This is often referred to as the fall back or bottom line.

Useful vocabulary

agree: zustimmen
disagree: nicht zustimmen
empower: befugen, bevollmächtigen
limits: Grenzen
meet halfway: auf halbem Weg entgegenkommen
mutually: gegenseitig
require: verlangen, voraussetzen

A negotiation agenda

During a negotiation it may be difficult to decide which topics are important to discuss and which are irrelevant. Establishing a negotiation agenda can render a discussion much more efficient for both sides. An agenda can be compared to the track a train runs on, as you travel through the negotiation. A negotiation agenda, unlike a meeting agenda, has specific content and an order that drives the negotiation forward.

Items of an agenda

An agenda includes the following items:

- Date, time and location of the meeting
- Names and titles of team members
- A general timescale for the period of negotiation
- The main issues to be addressed
- The proposed order

Example: Preliminary agenda

Meeting between IBL GmbH and TMA Inc.
At HES café, from 2 pm until 4 pm
Proposed new material for courses
Friday, 16 January 2011
Introductions by participants.
Agree on the meeting agenda.
Issues:
Who will use which material?
Which programme will pay the costs?
Who will be responsible during the trial runs?

How are the assessments done?
Refreshment break (HES café).
Who will present the outcomes?
What about digital aspects?
Summary of agreement.

Making an agenda will not only offer some structure to a negotiation, but it will also help you to identify your own priorities and goals and to compare these to those of you opponent. It will prevent an endless debate. The items on an agenda are usually called the "Heads of agenda". Drafting an agenda may contribute to a positive atmosphere, as it shows that you are looking for progress in the negotiation. It may also be seen as a first small agreement between parties.

Be careful not to reveal key aspects of your priorities, your preferences or your intended strategy in the agenda.

In more hostile relationships between negotiators, it helps to use less specific agenda headings (e.g.: "prices" instead of "price increases"), or perhaps even to only agree on an agenda as such, but to disagree on the order of the items. Especially when negotiating with international parties, it is wise to be flexible with the negotiation agenda.

Time limits

Negotiating can be an exhausting experience. Prepare to take proper breaks for coffee, lunch, dinner, sleep. Over and above these natural requirements, breaks or adjournments in the negotiation are very useful. Be aware that the other side may have a different perspective of time. "Time is money" is a common thought in North American minds, but time spent on socialising may influence others more.

Useful phrases

- I've drawn up an agenda.
- I hereby send you a copy of the revised agenda.
- Does the agenda meet your expectations? There are four items on the revised agenda.
- Are there any points you wish to add?
- We believe some points are missing.
- Is including point ... OK with you?
- Shall we include ... on the agenda after point 4?

Useful vocabulary

item on the agenda / agenda item: TOP (Tagesordnungspunkt)
agenda headings: Verhandlungsgegenstand, TOP
to be on the agenda: auf der Tagesordnung stehen
to delete from the agenda: von der Tagesordnung entfernen
circulate the agenda: die Agenda verteilen
chairman: Vorsitzender
AOB (any other business): „Sonstiges" als TOP
closure: Schließung
confine: eingrenzen
minutes: Protokoll
proceeding: fortführen
priority: Priorität, Vorrang

settled: entschieden
TBA (to be announced): wird angekündigt
timescale: Zeitplan, zeitlicher Rahmen
venue: Handlungsort

Promoting the climate

Being comfortable while negotiating is important. Sitting in a stuffy office without regular breaks or suffering from jet lag is detrimental to decision-making. One should be aware of creating a positive environment and working climate for the negotiations. If you are the host, make sure that you have comfortable rooms available. It's important to have space where parties can take a separate break to discuss privately.

The following aspects should be taken into account:

- A large comfortable room,
- A large table,
- Enough space to walk about,
- Material for presenting at hand,
- Discreet staff that prevent disturbances,
- Regular cleaning and serving of refreshments,
- Direct, secure telephones, internet access,
- Access to any equipment required, e.g. photocopiers, faxes, data projectors (beamers),
- Secure recess rooms for each team.

Ensure that you or someone else is in place to meet guests and make introductions. Doing this correctly is important in all cultures. People react better when they feel respected and looked after. Getting this right is not so easy. Many Europeans, for example, will become suspicious if they feel you are over-doing things, while many Asians will feel uneasy if they feel you are under-doing things.

Knowing the participants

It is important to find out exactly who you will be meeting with. What is that person's position in the company, and his/her decision-making powers? These matters may also influence the choice of venue, hotel bookings and even seating arrangements at the meeting itself. If it is possible to ask about the participants' preferences, this could be leading in, for instance, choosing refreshments or hotel bookings. An often overlooked issue is that national holidays differ substantially, which may influence the other party's travel arrangements.

Getting acquainted

The way people are welcomed, can influence the atmosphere substantially, as is illustrated in the following example;

Example: Wrong beginning

Delegates from Bangalore, India and Shenzhen, China arrive at Frankfurt airport, and are unpleasantly surprised by the fact that they weren't welcomed personally, but only received detailed (perfectly) written information. Such misunderstandings can influence the atmosphere negatively.

Greeting

First impressions are important. Research shows that during the first seconds of meeting individuals interpret the other person's character, mood, and even manner in how they are going to negotiate. We therefore need to give some thought as to how best present ourselves. This is also relevant when you have met the person or persons previously. The way you greet someone is a form of respect. Each culture has developed its own norms of greeting. Some are better than others at learning about another's greeting norms and being prepared for them. In most cultures of the world, seniority and hierarchy are important in whom to greet first.

Handshakes

Any face-to-face contact requires some handling. The English verb to handle is related to the word hand, and in most countries a handshake is the preferred way of greeting. In some countries a handshake is not acceptable, particularly between male and female, and in others, a bow is more appropriate.

Example: Handshakes with women

Handshakes with Iranian women aren't appreciated, whereas a lady from the Saudi delegation, for example, might shake your hand.

Additionally, there are subtle differences in how long a handshake should last. These may be mere seconds, as between European countries, but can last much longer further afield. A short handshake in some cultures means you're not to be trusted.

Welcoming words

In addition to a handshake, some welcoming words need to be said. Please note that the question "How do you do?" is best answered with "How do you do?" or "I'm fine, thank you. How are you?" A commonly made mistake by non-English speakers is to take such phrases seriously and reply in detail.

Example: Welcoming words

A: On behalf of Muster GmbH, I am very glad to welcome you to our Berlin office.

B: Joey, how are you?

A: Good to see you again, Horst. How are you?

B: Fine thanks. Have you met Anke?

C: Hello, I am Anke Laffort, responsible for international marketing at our Fraijlemaburg branch.

A: Nice to meet you Anke. How was your flight?

Below are some sample phrases for welcoming international guests.

Useful phrases

- Well, I'm delighted to welcome you all to our offices here in Düsseldorf.
- Thank you for coming, everyone.

- Welcome to Munich!
- I'm chairing ...
- On behalf of Muster GmbH, I am very glad to welcome you to our head office.
- It really is a pleasure for us to meet you all.
- How do you do?
- How are you?
- Nice to meet you.
- Hello ... Good to see you again.
- It is a pleasure to meet you, I'm ...

Introducing oneself and others

Having the greeting, handshake or bow, and welcoming words in place, how do we best introduce ourselves?

Names and titles

The easiest approach throughout the world when introducing yourself in English is to use your first name (or the name you generally use as your first name) and surname: "I'm John Smith, pleased to meet you." Listen to how the other party introduces itself. For example, in Britain, Ireland, the US and Australia they may only give you their first name: "Hi, I'm John, glad you could join us today." Some professions may continue to prefer the more formal surname: "Good afternoon, I'm Mr. Smith, partner solicitor in this firm." Certain professions such as doctors or professors continue to use their title: "Hello, I'm Dr. John Smith, from the orthopaedic department." If you have received correspondence in advance, letters or emails, they may give a clue as to how they would like to be addressed.

Useful phrases

- Let me introduce you to Mert Doğan. Mert's our key Account Manager.
- My name's Mert Doğan. I'm in charge of Corporate Affairs here in Estonia.
- Let me introduce you to Deshtan, who looks after our offices in Austria.
- Hello. I'm Ulrik Bisgaard, in charge of Marketing.
- I don't think you have met ...
- John, this is Marie Müller, Marketing Director at Sanflower in Munich.
- Nice to meet you. This is ... She's in charge of...
- Jürgen, would you like to introduce your team?
- Let me introduce you to Dr. Hans-Peter Uhl.

Job positions

Stating your job position in the company differs from country to country. For example, in the UK, people may be shy about indicating their job title. John's title is General Manager of Sales Department but he is more likely to introduce himself as: "I'm John from Hounslow Engineering." In the US, job titles are very important so they will usually specify: "I'm Joe, vice president of Sales, Houston Engineering." In China or

Japan people may give you their company name, followed by department, job title and finally their name.

- I'm from Donghua Daxui, the International Department.
- I'm the vice Dean, and my name is Frances Liu.

Morc spccific job titles or positions may be:

- I'm the exclusive representative for....
- I'm one of the many local sales teams.
- My company is in the field of ...
- I'm commissioned by ...
- I have been given the power of attorney for...

Business cards

A lot has been written on how to receive a business card. For example, that it is important to study them respectfully instead of simply sticking someone's card into your pocket, or that in Asian cultures, people give and receive cards with both hands. Very little, however, has been written on what information is written on cards and their actual appearance.

Example: Business cards

In a country like South Korea someone's job description is considered very important, or in France people may add extra information.

In many cultures a card is simply something practical, containing contact information, but there are also cultures where much more attention is given to the quality of the material or the printing technique. It is logical that when visiting such countries you want to pay some attention to such details. Finally, it is advisable to have your business card translated on the reverse of your card in cultures where English is less commonly spoken. For example, if travelling to South Korea, have a Korean translation on the reverse. It is advisable to have your business card translated into English on the reverse when travelling to English-speaking countries, unless it is clear to non-German speakers. Being confronted with a business card in another language makes many English speakers uneasy.

> Take enough time to have the translations and proofs double-checked by native speakers from the target country itself. Too many companies have made silly bloopers without knowing it.

Addressing others

For many English-speaking cultures, first names have become the usual way of introduction. It feels very formal and pompous to give your full name such as Mr. Smith unless in a specific job such as Dr. Smith. Thus, when doing business with Americans, Australians, New Zealanders, Canadians, British, South Africans or Irish, it may surprise you, how quickly they can switch to using first names. Many East Asian countries (China, Japan, South Korea) reverse the order so the surname comes first. This is a difficult hurdle for any cultural group to overcome, so we tend to find ourselves being called Mr Stefan instead of Mr Aust and we refer to them as Mr Jintao instead of Mr Hu. East Asians prefer to be more formal initially, particularly when older people are concerned. They are uncomfortable using first names and also nicknames.

People from cultures that use family names in combination with Mr and Mrs may feel a bit uneasy. Nevertheless, it is important to think about the social consequences of not being on first-name terms with people. It may seem too distant or even unfriendly. Therefore, simply follow the approach of your conversation partner. And note that it may sound somewhat strange to suggest "dozen", as this option does not exist in English between "Du" and "Sie"; both mean "you".

Many Americans or other English-speaking people commonly use nicknames in their business contacts. The English language often shortens first names.

Example: Common nicknames

Examples of common nicknames are: Harry (Harold), Tony (Anthony), Bob (Robert), Gene (Eugene), Jack (John), Bill (William), Frank (Francis) and Ted (Edward).

To address business partners with their full first name could look somewhat strange. Some people will even mention their nickname on their business card (in quotation marks), for example: Robert "Chip" Loeffler. Their first name will naturally appear in full on most judicial documents. It is not uncommon for people to be known by another name other than their first in the British Isles. For example, Francis Gordon

Lacey is known to everyone as Gordon except on official documents.

Socialising and small talk

For the majority of cultures, socialising in the work environment plays an important, sometimes vital role. Getting to know the person you are doing business with is as important as the actual business itself. In most of the Arab cultures it is practically impossible to do business without knowing the person very well. Leaving room for getting to know people is an important element in any negotiation.

Small talk is used both to get to know other people, as well as help put people at ease. Some cultures place more emphasis on this than others, but it's important at all times. Always begin with small talk even if late for a meeting. Never begin with business. If you arrive in the middle of a meeting, apologise even if it's not your fault for being late before you make your business points. If you start immediately with business, you are in danger of being thought of as anything between nervous to rude to downright dangerous.

Small-talk items

What is discussed during small talk is generally not business-related. This comes naturally to many people, but can be an issue for others. Items such as the weather, your journey to the meeting and sports are often the only topics mentioned, as they are usually non-controversial. Americans are happy to talk about their families in detail but other English-speaking cultures tend to keep family private. Talking about family is vital to cultures that need to build a relationship, such as certain Asian, Middle Eastern, African and South American countries as they need to have an overview of your family and your role in the family group. However, you do not have to go into great detail.

Politics, cultural differences, sex and religion are best avoided unless you already know they can be discussed. If these come up at any time during negotiations then it's best to be curious and open, rather than state opinions. Health is a subject most English-speaking cultures talk freely about. It is important to show sympathy with any illnesses mentioned, even if you may think they're purely psychological.

> "Let's get down to business" is a signal many use as the reference moment when enough small talk has taken place. It is best to try to feel the atmosphere before proceeding too quickly. You want to avoid making the other side feel uncomfortable.

How it works

Small talk is used in English speaking cultures to influence conversations in a positive way. Small talk is functional to introduce or end a conversation with a few phrases about friendly and risk-free topics. It helps to create a polite and friendly atmosphere. Try to use open questions (see section on Asking questions). It is also possible to answer a question with another question if you don't want to respond to the question asked.

Useful phrases

- How was your journey?
- How was the flight over?
- Is your hotel comfortable?
- Is everything all right with the hotel?
- Is this your first visit to Germany?
- Would you like anything to drink?
- You must be jet-lagged after such a long flight.
- Would you like me to order some coffee?
- How's the weather in France at the moment?
- How was your break in France?
- How's business in your sector?

Opening phase

All negotiations have an established procedural structure, regardless of the various partners or topics. The phases of negotiating we distinguish in this book are:

- Preparation and planning phase
- Opening phase
- Main phase
- Agreement phase

Although these phases are distinct, they do not necessarily have to follow the described sequence.

Example: Phases of negotiating

An offer sent by way of an email campaign, would already start in phase three: the main phase, whereas an interested recipient of the mail might want to look into the details of the product (i.e. the preparation and planning phase).

This implies that the main reason for identifying the four negotiation phases isn't that they are consecutive, but the fact that they ask for different skills. And whether we are aware or ignorant of these different phases: they all require specific behaviour. And that's something that comes of course with its own specific language requirements. The important elements of the preparation and planning phase have already been discussed in the previous chapter; we therefore concentrate here on what happens during the actual negotiation.

Once the socialising and small talk has taken place, the negotiation can begin. For smooth negotiations, the following steps are useful in the beginning:

- State the purpose of the negotiation.
- Agree on the agenda.
- State your interests.
- Listen to the other party's interests.
- Clarify anything unclear or incorrect.

Stating the purpose

Why are you negotiating? This may seem obvious, but it's surprising how often parties discover during a negotiation they are not discussing the same purpose. Stating clearly the purpose of the negotiation provides the basic framework for everyone. One of the most important moments in a negotiation is explaining your interests and what you hope to achieve. It is better to lay down what you want from the beginning. The first information discussed has a great influence in determining the outcome.

Example: Stating the purpose

We are here to discuss the acquiring of land for the purpose of constructing a petrol station and shop. Our desire is to be able to agree today on a satisfactory price for all concerned and achieve a timetable for planning operations with all the relevant stakeholders.

Objective criteria are the accepted standards between the parties, as to how all parties can fairly judge the outcome of the agreement. This could be market price, government regulation, precedent, local trading conditions, fairness or anything which all parties can accept. There may be more than one criterion. It is important that all the parties agree because without an agreed objective criterion there is no basis for an agreement.

Example: Objective criteria

The petrol station and shop are to be built between a motorway and an office building. The building regulations for foundations, distance from other buildings and from the road are strict. There is no point for the owner to sell the land to a buyer if he cannot meet such regulations. The objective criteria could thus be based on both price as well as the specific regulations.

Useful phrases

Below are some useful phrases a chairperson can use.

- Could I have your attention, please?
- OK, everyone, sorry to interrupt, but we are short of time, so let's get started.
- Ladies and gentlemen, we have a rather full agenda, so perhaps we had better get down to business.
- Shall we just go round the table, making sure we all know each other?
- OK, we've called this meeting in order to ...
- We're here today to try and reach an agreement about two items: payment terms and the penalty clause.
- As you know, we're here today to discuss ...
- The prime objective of our meeting today should be to agree ... .

Useful vocabulary

framework: Rahmen
acquire: erwerben
stakeholders: Hauptinteressenten
criterion: Kriterium, Maßstab
to get down to business: beginnen, anfangen
the objectives of the meeting: Ziele der Verhandlung
to fill somebody in on something: informieren

The agenda

The phrases below can be functional in getting participants to agree on a prepared agenda.

Useful phrases

- Firstly, can I suggest we start by taking a look at the agenda we have sent you?
- Today we will discuss some difficult points; therefore I'd like to suggest we try and stick to a meeting procedure.
- We have drawn up an agenda which covers the main areas for negotiation today. Are you happy about all this?
- Did everyone receive a copy of the agenda from Ms Bakridi?
- Let me inform you of the sequence of negotiation topics.
- On the agenda today we have ..., are there any comments on this?
- There are six items on the agenda. First ..., second ..., third ..., lastly .... Does your party agree that we take these points in this order?
- Your agenda allocates five minutes for this item, but we believe ...
- Diederik, could you bring us up to date on item three on the agenda?

Useful vocabulary

to delete from the agenda: von der Tagesordnung nehmen
to be on the agenda: auf der Tagesordnung stehen

Main phase

Now that the preliminaries are out of the way and the opening points have been stated, the train has left the station and the negotiation is moving along at its own speed. All the elements of negotiation planning, experience, and tactics come to life here. We take you through some of the most relevant aspects and give some suggestions on how to approach using appropriate English. Since asking questions, listening and dealing with people are so important we have placed them in separate sections.

Bargaining

Bargaining means to negotiate, argue, or barter about the terms of a business transaction, usually focussing on the purchase or selling price of a product or service. It therefore requires a party that has something to offer as an exchange. English speakers are very familiar with the terms "hard" and "soft" approach. Usually they add the term sell or bargaining as in "hard sell" or "hard bargaining". They might believe they're going to "drive a hard bargain" or make it seem like a "soft sell". All of these force the negotiation towards a win-lose outcome despite everyone stating they want a win-win situation. Parties need each other; otherwise they would not be negotiating. Acknowledging this allows you to focus on the solution of what is on the table. Give and take, making concessions is required. Without these, stalemate can ensue which means nothing further happens. Making a concession can break the stalemate and move the discussions further towards an agreement, a win-win.

Price discussions

Bargaining predominates in one-time negotiations and often revolves around a single issue, usually the price. In lots of business cultures people are used to a higher degree of bargaining than in northern Europe. In such cultures the first offer is usually substantially higher or lower than the final offer in a negotiation.

Example: Price discussions

A: What discount could you give us on a larger order?

B: That depends, how many units you were thinking of?

A: We would like to buy something in the ballpark of fifteen units.

B: Okay. Well, if you were to order twenty units, I'd be willing to give you nine percent off the list price.

A: I understand, and what kind of a discount can we get on fifteen units?

B: Not that much, probably around four percent.

A: That means with the three percent for prompt payment, we are talking about seven percent off your list price. I'm afraid that's a bit of a stretch, I could agree to an offer of nine percent.

B: That seems high to me, Horst. Can you go a little lower?

A: Your changing the price by nine percent would enable us to seriously consider the deal.

B: You drive a hard bargain; I'd like to consult head office before committing.

Zone of possible agreement

In order to achieve agreement at a certain stage, you will need to have an idea of the other party's area or zone of agreement. The image below shows us that the buyer is willing to pay between 1,000 € (minimum) and 3,500 € (maximum), and the seller is asking for a minimum of 3,000 € and a maximum of 5,000 € in their respective settlement areas. The buyer and seller and agree on a price somewhere between 3,000 € and 3,500 €. This is known as the zone of possible agreement (ZOPA). Until parties are negotiating in ZOPA, they will be unable to come to an agreement.

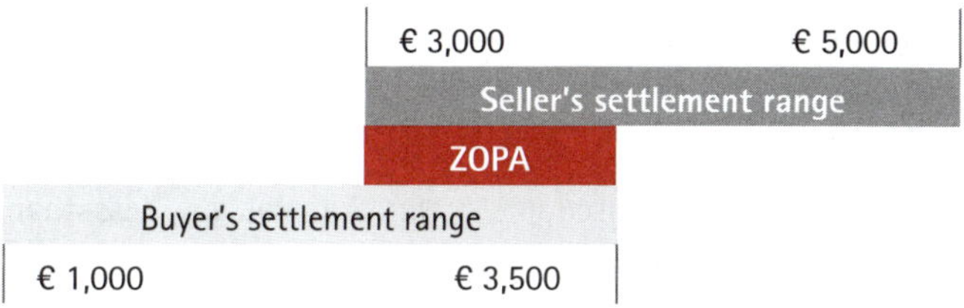

Useful phrases

- Can we talk about the price?
- Is this price negotiable?
- Is there a possibility you could move closer to our quoted price?
- Is that your best offer?
- What room for manoeuvre do you have here?
- We could offer you a slight reduction on certain conditions of course.

- We could reduce the prices in exchange for a guarantee on quantity.
- What would you say if we offered you …?
- I'm afraid we will have to look elsewhere, unless …
- We will increase our offer by …
- We could alter the payment terms, would that do?
- We will cover the rate of interest, okay?
- If you pay in ten days, we will abate the payment terms.
- If you sign the contract now, we'll improve the payback period as you suggested.
- Could I ask you how much you had in mind?

Price reductions

Price reductions or discounts mean that you pay less than the regular or list price. If orders are incomplete or incorrect, negotiators can also ask for discounts. It might take some creative preparation; therefore the overview below lists a selection of reasons for asking for price deductions.

- Early payment
- Advance payment
- Payment of a deposit
- Purchase of several items
- Use of name in supplier advertising
- Order of large volumes
- End of stock purchase

- First of stock purchase
- Recommendation to other customers
- Loyalty to supplier over the years
- First-time use of supplier
- Placing all business with the supplier
- Delivery at unusual times
- Instant or delayed delivery
- Collecting ex-works (with own transport)

Useful vocabulary

price proposal: Preisvorschlag
high/low-priced: hoch/niedrigpreisig
to undercut somebody's prices: jemanden unterbieten
pricing factors: preisbestimmende Faktoren
to limit a price: Preislimit setzen
asked or asking price: geforderter Preis
authority to negotiate: die Befugnis zu verhandeln
something in the ballpark of: ungefähr
prompt payment: prompte, termingerechte Zahlung
drive a hard bargain: hart verhandeln
proposal for amendment: Änderungsvorschlag
settlement: Einigungsvorschlag
to submit proposals: Vorschläge unterbreiten
to carry on negotiations for a settlement: Vergleichsverhandlungen fortführen
counterproposal: Gegenvorschlag
open to negotiations: verhandlungsbereit

to take up negotiations: Verhandlungen aufnehmen
to refer back: verweisen auf

Having looked at the preliminary and exploration phase of negotiating, the next paragraphs will concentrate on some practical negotiation skills, such as how to mark transitions, or how to summarise the other party's propositions, and the how and why of adjourning during a negotiation.

Marking transitions

There are many ways to indicate a transition in an argumentative talk, for instance by gestures or changes in tone or volume, but because this may differ from culture to culture, it is often advised to mark transitions in words when negotiating internationally. The phrases below offer some examples for this:

Useful phrases

- I'd like to expand on that a little before we move on.
- Let me point out here that ...
- Now here's one more fact about ...
- What I'd like to focus on here is ...
- Let's look more closely at ...
- After this general look, let's now turn to specific issues.
- That was an overview; now let's look at some details.
- Let me first give you a brief overview.

Linking words

Linking words help to connect ideas and sentences, so that people can follow what is said more easily. Your advantage of using specific linking words or expressions is that they can give the people sitting at the conference table a better idea of the structure of your line of reasoning. The overview below offers some alternatives.

Making conditions

Use one of the following expressions to insist on something:

- If
- Until
- Unless
- Provided

Reiterating propositions

Use one of the following expressions for repeating:

- To reiterate
- Altogether
- In short
- To reconsider
- All in all
- In particular
- On the whole
- To recount

Additional arguments

When you want to add an extra argument or reason, it sounds nicer not only to use words like "and" or "also" but to vary a bit. The table below offers some alternatives:

- Furthermore, ...
- Additionally, ...
- Moreover, ...
- ...as well as ...

- In addition, ...
- Besides, ...
- What is more, ...
- On another point, ...

Overview

When you want to give an overview of the points mentioned, you can indicate this by using the following expressions:

- To conclude, ...
- Summarising, ...
- In other words, ...
- All in all, ...
- Finally, ...
- To sum it up, ...
- To recap it briefly, ...
- In brief, ...
- Most important, ...
- In conclusion, ...

Emphasising statements

Use one of the following linking words to accentuate things:

- Certainly
- Of course
- In fact
- Indeed

Providing an example

Use one of the following expressions to illustrate something:

- For instance
- To put it another way
- For example
- More specifically
- To illustrate
- In other words
- As an example
- To be exact

Linking conflicting facts

Use one of the words below to combine conflicting facts:

- On the other hand
- However
- In reality
- Nonetheless
- On the contrary
- In contrast

Interrupting

Getting your point across or interrupting the other person or people speaking can be delicate. Latin Americans and southern Europeans tend to be comfortable with talking over each other. Avoid beginning too directly, but use softening words instead such as those listed here.

Useful phrases

- Excuse me for interrupting, but ...
- I'd like to comment on that.
- Sorry to interrupt, but perhaps the members of the board would like to know more about our ... ?
- Could I just say one thing?
- I'm glad you brought that up, Bill.
- Could I just come in here?
- In my opinion this counter-offer is ...
- It's also worth noting that ...
- Mister, Madam Chairman?

Rephrasing

Rephrasing is an important tool for negotiators, as it allows them to express ideas in different, perhaps more acceptable ways. It can also prevent misunderstandings during negotiations with non-native speakers of English.

Useful phrases

- So, let's just recap on that.
- Sorry, what we actually meant (to explain) is this ...
- Basically, what our side is saying is this ...
- Earlier on I wasn't clear about our counter-offer.
- What my colleague is saying is that ... .
- My client would like to recap on the main points.
- I'd like to digress here for a moment and mention that ...
- Sorry, perhaps I didn't make the additional demand clear.
- I'm afraid I'm not quite clear what you mean.
- Sorry, I'm not sure I understood. Would you mind going over that again?
- Correct me if I'm wrong, but ...
- Did I get it right that ...?
- The point I'm making is that ...

Useful vocabulary

contradiction: Widerspruch, Gegensatz
dissent: Unstimmigkeit, Meinungsverschiedenheit
opposites: Gegensätze

by mutual agreement: im gegenseitigen Einvernehmen
counter-offer: Gegenangebot
to recap: kurz zusammenfassen
to digress: abschweifen von

Referring back

Use one of the following phrases to refer back to earlier mentioned discussion points.

Useful phrases

- To refer back to an earlier point, ...
- Let's go back to what you were offering earlier.
- Let me go back to the cost break down of ...
- Taking into consideration what Mrs Porath-Funk said ...
- I'd like to return to what you were proposing earlier.
- Let's go back to the question of possible alternatives.
- To go back to what you said earlier ...
- Let's look back for a moment.

Making your point clear

You will want to get your points across to the other side; otherwise coming to an agreement will be hard to achieve. Phrasing the sentence in reference to yourself takes any offence, discomfort, or loss of face away from the other parties. You take ownership for the opinion or information this way.

Useful phrases

- I really think it would be better to ...
- The way I see things ...
- From my perspective ...
- Well, in our opinion, ...
- In my (professional) opinion ...
- In my experience ...
- Past experience has taught me that ...
- If you look at it from our point of view, then ...
- What you're saying is that you ...
- That's not exactly how I look at it.
- I think this proves the point that ...
- Well, personally, I think the best solution is ...
- I feel that ...
- I suggest that we should ...
- Therefore, it is clear that ...
- I think it's obvious that ...

Summarising

Summarising is a vital negotiating technique when so much has been said and interruptions have occurred. A summary can refocus attention on the issues at hand, particularly when not negotiating in your mother tongue. Summaries are of necessity in certain cultures.

Example: Summaries and different cultures

The Japanese will take it particularly seriously. English-speaking cultures tend to rush through this part, often referring to it as recapping, e.g. "Shall we recap before shaking hands?"

In general, you can say that summaries should be concise and neutral, and refer to one or more of the following elements:

- The different points covered,
- The proposals of each side,
- The discrepancies agreed between parties,
- What has been excluded,
- What is agreed upon.

Useful phrases

Use one of the following phrases to summarise points:

- To summarise, ...
- Let me quickly summarise the principal results.
- Let's summarise what is on the table.
- I'd like to go over the main points now.
- Let me briefly recap your suggested options.
- The pros and cons were as follows ...
- In addition to that, outstanding issues are ...
- There is still the question of ... to resolve.
- To sum up, we have made progress with the ...

- Parties have agreed the following ...
- Is there anything you wish to add?
- Is this an accurate summary?

Useful vocabulary

to give a summary: eine Zusammenfassung geben
recapitulation: Zusammenfassung
to recap: rekapitulieren
a concise explanation: präzise Darlegung
divergence of opinion: Meinungsverschiedenheit

Adjourning

To adjourn means to suspend proceedings to another time or place. Depending on the circumstances, adjournments can be for a few minutes, a couple of hours or even a few weeks. In certain negotiations, it may be constructive to take a break or adjourn a meeting. Usually this is the case in one of the circumstances mentioned below:

- To digest new important information received,
- To consult or obtain instructions from decision makers,
- To regroup a negotiation team,
- To diffuse tension,
- To counteract pressure from the other side that is pushing for a decision,
- When coming close to the least acceptable position,
- When being close to a deal,
- Or simply because people are getting tired.

Example: Adjourning

Chairman: "We have summarised the benefits for you of accepting the offer on the table. I propose that we adjourn, while each party consults its advisers. Can we then reconvene at 4 pm., to indicate acceptance or otherwise?"

Useful phrases

- If there are no further comments, we will adjourn the meeting here.
- I just have a few closing remarks and then you will all be free to go for lunch.
- It is getting too personal. Can I suggest we take a break?
- We propose adjourning and reconvening at two o'clock.
- Before we adjourn this meeting, let me just summarise the main items.
- Shall I go over the main points?
- Let's bring things to a close for this part of the negotiation.
- I'm afraid we're going to have to cut this meeting short.
- I think we'll wrap up this last point, and take a break.
- Well, we have even finished ahead of schedule.
- If no one has anything else to add, then I guess that will be all for today.

Useful vocabulary

to adjourn sine die: sich auf unbestimmte Zeit vertagen („sine die" = lat. für „ohne Tag")
closing: Schließung

concession: Zugeständnis
stalemate situation: Pattsituation
to come to a deadlock: ergebnislos verlaufen, stecken bleiben

Agreement phase

Research shows that in the last ten percent of the meeting time, approximately ninety percent of negotiations get settled. Sometimes negotiating parties miss the moment of agreement, simply because they do not pay attention to the atmosphere at the table. The right moment for agreement has come when:

- The differences between parties have become small,
- One party really stops making concessions,
- You have reached your prepared targets,
- You start reaching your own deadline.

Reaching an agreement

Now the train is pulling into the station and you want to step off with a successful result. Before making an agreement (closing a deal), think over the situation carefully.

- Will it achieve your goal; does it cover all your interests?
- Is it within you parameters?
- Is it better than your alternative (BATNA, see page 9)?

Once you are happy to agree on a final offer and close the deal, you want to be sure this is actually happening. Double check to be sure everyone is in agreement. Think about how the other parties may perceive the outcome.

Example: Reaching an agreement

The Scandinavians, Czechs and Dutch will be more in line with your own thinking about the long-term elements. The British will have a more flexible approach to future issues, the Americans prefer all important elements to be covered in the contract, and those cultures that are relationship-based, will focus on how everyone is reacting to the issues being agreed.

Whether the follow-up of an agreement will be called a contract or not, a good agreement represents the result of what has been negotiated, in a mutually acceptable form. English-speaking countries do not distinguish the type of agreement. Whether it's a simple or very complicated agreement it is classed in the same manner. Some sectors have their own specific agreement formats or legal requirements.

- A draft agreement would mean you have not reached a final agreement and it is temporary.
- A preliminary agreement is the basis for a more extensive final agreement and although it is not 100% confirmation, it does provides comfort that a final agreement will be made.
- A non-disclosure agreement means that one or more parties to the agreement must not divulge the information (or part of) to anyone else.

Useful phrases

- I believe both parties can agree to these terms.
- Can we agree to what we have proposed jointly?
- I propose that we leave it this way for the moment.
- Can we set about implementing our agreement as it now stands?
- We've been brainstorming back and forth over this issue for some minutes now, but it really sounds like we've found some common ground here.
- Can you agree to the adaptation of the written proposal?
- We would need to see some movement on price.
- Can we agree to what we have proposed jointly, and set about implementing our agreement as it now stands?
- This is our final offer.
- Can your client agree to the second proposal?

Ensuring agreement

Some useful sentences are provided here to help with ensuring that you are in agreement:

- Well, I think we've both agreed on the terms. Can we shake on it?
- I think we should get this in writing.
- We can certainly agree to this new counter-proposal.
- We agree on this particular clause in the contract.

- We agree with you, as far as this is concerned.
- By mutual agreement we have decided that ....
- We feel exactly the same way.
- We agree with you, as far as this is concerned.
- We can accept that.
- That's right / correct / possible.
- I certainly agree to that.
- We feel exactly the same way.
- We agree on this matter.
- I couldn't agree with you more.
- I agree with you entirely.
- That sounds like a very good idea to me.

Useful vocabulary:

to agree on: sich einigen über
as agreed upon: wie vereinbart
unless otherwise agreed: soweit nichts anderes vereinbart ist
agreed price fixing: Preisabsprache
to come to an agreement: eine Einigung erzielen
to reach an agreement on the price: sich über den Preis einigen
to decide upon concerted action: sich zu einem gemeinsamen Vorgehen entschließen

Disagreeing

You may find that you cannot agree with the proposals and need to find a suitable way to let this be known. Directness is not to be used. Asian and Latin Americans may lose face. The British will be uncomfortable at the least. Saying no doesn't work in some cultures. Even saying yes does not necessarily mean you agree. Yes from a Japanese means: "Yes, I hear you." not: "Yes, I agree". Therefore some softening of the information by using extra apologetic wording is required. The sentences below are listed in the order of least confrontational to most confrontational to English speakers:

Useful phrases

- We're afraid we'd have to disagree about that.
- We're not sure we agree with that.
- This isn't quite what we were expecting.
- We may have to disagree.
- That's probably not possible for us.
- This is missing some details.
- I'm afraid my management cannot accept the proposed explanation in this form.
- I tend to disagree because....
- I'm sorry, but I can`t agree because.....
- I beg to differ.
- I'm afraid we cannot accept your statement because....
- We don't agree on that because... .

- That's all very well but....
- With all due respect, I disagree on....
- Please do not misunderstand me but.....
- I don't wish to be rude but....

Useful vocabulary:

in the event of disagreement: falls keine Einigung zustande kommt
to contradict: widersprechen
to express disapproval: Missbilligung aussprechen

We agree, but...

Just about the moment you think agreement has been reached, you hear something like: "Your offer is acceptable, but there is just this small detail". When you have met their points to reach an agreement, another small detail appears again. What strategies can you implement to deal with this? Try techniques like the two examples below:

Example: Strategies

1: Are there any other issues you still have, if I may ask? Then I suggest that we first try to consider them together in a package.

2: We cannot really accept any changes on this small detail; however, if you were to adjust point ..., we can consider the change you suggested.

No subdivided agreement

In most cases, there are many rounds of negotiations. The preliminary round may uncover the major issues, while subsequent rounds may be needed to resolve them. Many issues will have been raised and either agreed upon or set aside for one or another reason. It is advisable not to agree to finalised parts of the negotiation separately. Always try instead to include all issues in one final agreement. This way, you will keep more space to manoeuvre. This can be best said as follows: "I agree to the proposal subject to the final agreement".

Closing remarks and next steps

It is necessary to indicate to the participants that negotiations have come to a close. Having come to an agreement, it is time to finalise. Depending on the importance of the agreement it may be a handshake, a signing ceremony and/or celebratory drinks. It is unwise to depart as soon as the agreement is reached. Most cultures require some form of recognition. For simpler agreements, a lot of handshaking and smiling should be enough. Americans, Australians and Latin Americans may even slap you on the back.

Useful phrases

- Our meeting today has been very productive.
- I think we have made excellent progress today.
- Our meeting today has given us a lot to think about.

- I suggest that we address the matter of clarifying the contingency sum again in our next meeting.
- Shall we meet again once we have had some time to consider the options?
- Can we set the date for the next meeting, please?
- We'll meet again on the twenty-seventh of next month, same time.
- We'll draft a detailed summary before the next meeting.
- I'll send out an email with the minutes in two days.
- The next step is to draft a formal contract.
- If anyone has any questions about what we agreed today, feel free to send me an email.
- It simply remains for me to thank you all for attending.
- I declare the meeting closed.
- We will send you the missing documents/deeds.
- We will take care of the formulating of the contract.
- Thank you all for your participation.

Useful vocabulary

successful conclusion of negotiations: erfolgreicher Abschluss einer Verhandlung
to contract for: sich vertraglich verpflichten
contracting party: Vertragspartei
to award the contract: den Auftrag vergeben
to receive the contract: den Zuschlag erhalten
contract in writing: schriftlicher Vertrag

to conclude a contract: einen Vertrag schließen
set the date: einen Termin festlegen
for your comments: zur Stellungnahme
to call it a day: Schluss machen, beenden

Asking questions

Asking questions to confirm what has been said or to clarify the information given can be extremely useful, as it helps to avoid misunderstandings. This is particularly important if the information is complicated, or when the parties do not know each other well, especially during cross-cultural negotiations, or when one or more of those attending are not native English speakers.

Clarifying

This section looks at how to clarify and evaluate positions when asking questions during a negotiation. It is important to achieve mutual understanding while trying to bring about an agreement. This is accomplished by making both your own team's position clear, as well as by understanding the other side's point of view concerning the offers or positions at hand. Try to avoid wording questions that are a direct challenge to the other person's position. It is clever to avoid questions like "If you want ... how can you also expect ... ?" or "Did you not say that ... ?"

Confirming questions

- Am I right in thinking that ... ?
- Could I just go over your main points again?
- In other words, you're interested in developing ... ?
- Did I understand correctly that what your board of management is saying concerns ... ?
- If I understand you correctly, you are asking ...
- Am I right in thinking that your ...
- Correct me if I'm wrong. What I understand here is that you are asking ... ?
- From your point of view, you consider the only way to resolve the packaging is to ....
- You state that you will write 64 pages, but can you confirm this will actually be possible given the timescale?
- Is this a good summary of your position?

Asking for clarification

- I'm afraid I didn't quite catch that.
- I'm sorry, could you simplify / rephrase your point?
- If I understood you correctly, you would like to ask ... ?
- I'm sorry. I don't quite understand the meaning of ....
- I'm afraid I don't see the connection here.
- Sorry, I'm not really sure what you mean.
- Could you go over that again?
- Do you mind me asking ... ?

Question categories

In order to understand the other party's interests, it is important to obtain as much information as possible. The best method is to ask lots of questions. Using various types of questions helps to bring about a more complete view of the other party and draws them further into the negotiation. These help to increase your knowledge in order to enhance your strategy and find synergies and mutual gain.

Emotional questions

- How do you feel about ... ?
- What are your thoughts about ... ?
- Why is that so important to you?

Open questions

- When can we expect ... ?
- How can we deal with that problem ... ?
- Where does your information come from?
- How much would you be willing to offer?

Particular questions

- Why are you interested in our product specifically?
- Which other suppliers are you dealing with?
- Why is that particular deadline so important for you?

Ensuring questions

- Sorry to interrupt, but I would like to know more about ...
- Excuse me, may I ask how you arrived at these results?
- One question. How do you plan to ... ?
- You mentioned ..., can you expand on that?
- Could you clarify what you said about ... ?
- Could I go back to the point you made about ... ?
- I want to take you up on what you said earlier about ...
- My client is interested in your opinion about ...
- Do you want us to draft that before our next meeting?
- Could I have that in writing, please?

Example: Ensuring questions

A: I'd like to talk you through the various points, if that's OK?

B: Sure, go ahead.

A: Well, to start with, we think that the payment terms need adaptation to the prevailing Swiss conditions.

B: Just a minute, Horst. Could you clarify something for me?

A: Of course.

B: What exactly do you mean by "the Swiss conditions"?

C: Look, sorry to digress, but what we'd particularly like to ask you about are the payment terms.

A: Oh, right, OK. Well, what is it in particular that you want to know about the payment terms?

What-if questions

Using "what if" questions can be very helpful during negotiations because they elucidate potential negotiable issues.

What-if questions can be used for exploring possible settlements in a conflict or deadlock situation. Their advantage is that they also avoid laying responsibility on any party as they are considered a suggestion rather than a proposal.

Example: What-if questions

A: Well, to start with, we think that the payment terms need adaptation to the prevailing Swiss conditions.

C: Look, sorry to digress, but what we'd particularly like to ask you about, are the payment terms.

A: WHAT IF we were to consider delaying the payment deadlines, would that serve your interests?

- If you ..., what would it be?
- What if ... ?

Question the facts

A proven method to create negotiating opportunities is to ask questions about how the other party arrived at their proposal. Why did they make certain assumptions, based on which facts, how relevant were the applied criteria, how reliable were the sources used, etc.. By forcing your negotiation counterpart to explain the build-up of their proposal, you are sure to find material to strengthen your own position. Think of questions like:

- What data did they use to calculate these figures?
- Excuse me, may I ask how you arrived at this result?
- On which facts is this proposal based, if I may ask?

- Can I ask you: what forms the basis of the claim in paragraph three of the proposal?
- How did you calculate option C on page four, if I may be so bold as to ask?
- Could I ask what source this information comes from exactly?
- Aren't these figures possibly setting too high a valuation on it?

Avoiding asking questions

Recent research has shown that German negotiators have some of the lowest scores with respect to asking questions during negotiations compared to other cultures. On the other hand, they have a very high level of self-disclosure. Brazilian, French or Spanish business people tend to negotiate quite self-assertively or forcefully, using a high percentage of threats, warnings and even commands. Naturally, there is the danger of stereotyping people, but then again the described cultural differences are worthwhile considering when preparing for any negotiations in an international context.

The art of listening

Listening to the other party is one of the more important tools in understanding its requirements and obtaining a mutual agreement. Experienced negotiation teams appoint an extra team member, solely for observing the other party members. Having asked a question it is important to understand the re-sponse. Listening is not as easy as it seems. People often just listen to themselves or their colleagues, not the others involved. Especially when under the pressure of negotiating, listening gets harder since stress inhibits people from listening properly.

> Avoid searching for responses to what is being said, but rather try to understand the other party as it sees itself.

It is sometimes explained in a simple way: "People have two ears and one mouth; they should try and use them proportionally". Listening involves concentrating on what the person is actually saying and assessing his/her body language. Many people are not sure of what they actually want. Confirming and clarifying questions therefore helps to understand their perceptions, emotions and constraints. It is advisable to make these questions positive from the other party's point of view. In other words avoid saying anything that makes the other party defensive. On the other hand, it is not necessary to agree, because understanding is not the same as agreeing. Misunderstandings are a frequent source of the reasons for poor negotiations or failure of negotiations. A foreign language can be especially problematic. Body language is also more important to be aware of than in your own culture. Confirming and clarifying can help to overcome such issues.

Benefits of listening

- It improves what you have to say and offer,
- It allows you to find mutual solutions,
- It helps overcome language misunderstandings,
- It allows the other person to feel they have been taken seriously.

People have a need to be heard. A successful negotiation only occurs when all parties feel their interests have been listened to.

Useful phrases

The following phrases show that you are listening:

- Hm, I understand.
- That's very interesting.
- Right.
- Okay, thank you.

When things get tough

It is difficult enough to resolve tensions and conflicts, but it is particularly challenging when a foreign language is involved.

Reducing tension

Naturally participants in negotiations can be somewhat tense, especially when they are operating outside their own environment. Here are some ways to contribute to a positive atmosphere. Before the start of the meeting it helps to walk around a bit, and have some informal contact or small talk. Another technique is to use a more careful choice of words.

Choice of words

The examples below show you the difference between direct and indirect wording:

Direct	Indirect
impossible	difficult
never done	not normally done
contrary to company policy	without precedent
no way	not under the current circumstances
not very encouraging	disappointing

Other Techniques

Besides a careful choice of words, some other techniques can contribute to a positive atmosphere. For example:

- Help build up a positive climate,
- Listen to the reasoning of others,
- Respond to remarks,
- Have a sense of humour,
- Relate to common interests,
- Avoid a tense or too formal attitude.

Reading between the lines

Cultures that use indirect speech, which includes most of the English-speaking world, use wording that requires reading between the lines. This means searching for the important words in sentences spoken. The highlighted words in the following sentences show where the important information is:

- As I'm sure you appreciate, this is a **difficult situation**.
  Means: this is very serious.
- This sounds like a slight **problem**.
  Means: we have a problem.
- I'm **not** very **happy** with that.
  Means: they're very unhappy.
- I like the idea, **but** we should look at ...
  Means: they don't like the idea.
- That's **not** quite what I **meant**
  Means: that's not correct.

Useful phrases

- We should look at the benefits from both sides.
- It's in all our interests to resolve the problem.
- We're here to try and find answers for all parties.
- Let's try to focus on the positive aspects.

Anger management

People identify themselves with the negotiation and particularly the outcome. When things are not going well, they may start to display irrational behaviour. Sometimes people start shouting or banging the table. Some cultures find this more acceptable than others. These may be tactics to put you under pressure, but more often people are becoming upset because they feel their interests are slipping away from them. In order to successfully control emotions, the suppression of your own thoughts, perceptions and emotions is advisable. This is not easy. It helps to hold your emotions in check by focussing on the issue and not on yourself or the others involved. The authors Fisher and Ury use the term: "Separate the people from the problem".

Example: Separate the people from the problem

If someone blames you for something, do not respond negatively. Depending on what it's about, you may be able to accept what they say or disagree.

This allows the issue to stand on its own and the negotiations to move on.

Useful phrases

- Your point is interesting, can you tell us more?
- If you are opposed, what is it that you object to?
- We need you to fully understand our priorities.
- We were slightly annoyed by ..., do you feel the same way?
- We feel pressured on our side, and this seems to influence our trust in these negotiations. I believe we should do something about this.
- Perhaps we are misunderstanding the situation.

Dealing with impasses

One of the best ways of finding a route around an impasse is reviewing the situation from the other side's perspective. What would you need or want, if you were the other party? You may then be able to find some common ground to propose a suggestion for moving forward. Within your strategy you should have options available that could now be used, or you may take another route if you have thought out an alternative position. Throwing a new idea into the ring will have a ripple effect and a good chance of producing a breakthrough.

> Writing up the items of the agenda can sometimes unblock stalled negotiations. This entails making a short list of areas to discuss. They do not need to be in a set order and shouldn't be presented as proposals.

Useful phrases

- How can we find a compromise for this?
- May I just explain our point of view?
- Your position is a different approach; can you tell us more?
- I think I see what you're getting at. Can I suggest a break; I would like to talk this through with my team.

Tables, graphs or charts

People in today's business community are so accustomed to the use of computerised visual aids that this can also be relevant for negotiations. The paragraphs hereunder give you an overview of the necessary key phrases. Having facts and figures at hand in a negotiation may strengthen one's position. There are many graphs or charts available in spreadsheet programs such as Excel and they all have their own specific use. The table below lists an overview of their names and German translations:

German	English
Baumdiagramm	tree diagram
Bilddiagramm	pictogram
Diagramm	diagram
Flussdiagramm	flowchart
gestrichelte Linie	a broken line
grünes Dreieck	green triangle
Histogramm	histogram

German	English
Säulendiagramm	bar chart *
Kreisdiagramm	pie chart
Kurve, Graph	graph
durchgezogene Linie	a solid line
Punktlinie	a dotted line
Schaubild	chart
schraffiertes Rechteck	shaded box
Tabelle	table
X-Achse, Y-Achse	x-axis, y-axis

* Note that (bar) graphs in American English are mostly called (bar) charts in British English.

Useful phrases

- I'd like to illustrate this by showing you ...
- The horizontal axis represents ...
- Each line on this second graph features ...
- The red shaded box here shows ...
- The blue dotted line gives us ...

Explaining graphs

Tables, graphs or charts can clarify situations, developments and processes, which would otherwise take a long time to explain in words. Visuals reduce the talking you have to do, which is of course easier when you need to negotiate in a foreign language.

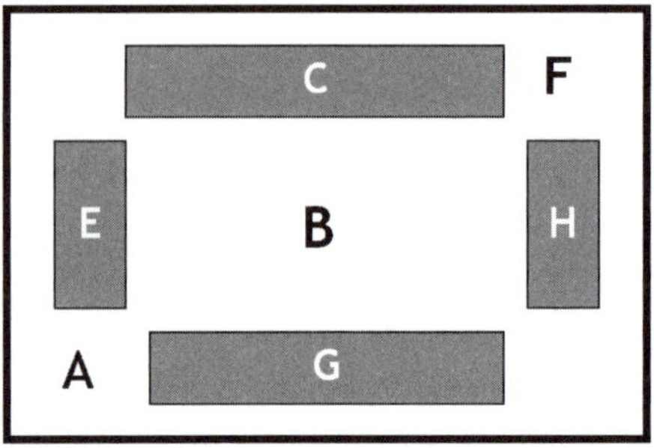

A. In the bottom left-hand corner or:
Down the left side of the chart

B. In the centre

C. Across the top

E. On the left

F. In the upper right-hand corner

G. Across the bottom

H. On the right

Useful phrases

- What you can see across the top is ...
- In the right-hand corner you will see ...
- Let us look at the upper half of the chart.
- But our chart shows a significant rise / dramatic increase in the number of ...
- Last year the number of ... went up sharply.
- Can you explain this trough in your graph?
- But your graph falls gradually after July.

- There has been a significant decrease in the number of ...
- We can see that the number of returns has stabilised / has reached a plateau / has levelled out.

Telephone negotiating

It is not always possible to meet face-to-face, but with the improvement of technical possibilities many companies nowadays prefer conference calls or video conferencing over long flights and hotel stays. There are still some points that make taking part in a telephone negotiation different from an ordinary meeting. First of all nonverbal communication isn't possible over a telephone, and ironic remarks in particular need facial expression. Another point is that not everybody will recognise each other's voices. Therefore it can be practical to mention one's name before talking. This is also helpful for the person taking the minutes.

When attending a conference call, it is important to understand English phrases and expressions related to such meetings. Also practical skills like keeping to the agenda, or knowing how to refocus, are components of an effective telephone negotiation. This may sound simple in German, but it requires some preparation in another language.

Example 1: Telephone negotiating

Thank you for dialling in today and welcome. My name is Wil Hazelhoff, I'm the chairperson of this conference call and I would like to welcome you all as participants to our telephone meeting. Let me start by reminding you that our call ends around 12 am. I would also like to inform you that the necessary conference documentation is called "ibl.doc". I will now quickly introduce you to all the other participants. May I ask you to greet the other members after your name is mentioned? This allows us to check that everyone is connected properly and that the technology is working smoothly. Thank you.

Then I would like to welcome Mr. Erik Borst from Freiburg, Germany. He will update us on the latest ICT Service bulletins and will be available for questions afterwards. May I then ...

Useful phrases

Beginning a telephone negotiation

- Let me inform you of the sequence of discussion topics.
- There are four items on the agenda. First ..., second ..., third ..., lastly ... Shall we take these points in this order?
- If you have a comment, please introduce yourself by name.
- Could you please indicate when you need to leave the phone for a short time, and mention your name?
- We have to end this conference call before the end of the hour.

During a telephone negotiation

- I know most of you, but there are a few unfamiliar voices.
- As chair, I'd like to take a moment to introduce Claudia.
- Let's quickly go through the minutes from the previous meeting. Claudia, can I put you in charge of reviewing the minutes from the last meeting for us?
- We cannot speak all at once, please.

Ending a telephone negotiation

- I think we've covered everything on the agenda.
- Shall we summarise the points of agreement?
- I will send the proposal to you for your comments.
- Before we close this meeting, let me just summarise the main items.
- Again, thank you all for taking time out of your busy schedules to be present.

Useful vocabulary

conference call: Telefonkonferenz, Sammelgespräch
audio recording: Tonaufnahme
summary: Zusammenfassung
connected: angeschlossen
bottom line: Fazit, letztes Angebot

Example 2: Telephone negotiating

A: Well, hello, everyone. My name is Bert, I am the Director at the Amsterdam office and I'm chairing today's meeting. We've organised this conference call to collectively decide by vote on Frankfurt's proposition. I hope you've all had a chance to look at Nasma's report. I suggest we go in the same order as our last meeting and each say what we think, and afterwards we will vote. Wil, what is your opinion on the proposal?

B: Wil speaking. Thank you. Personally, I think the best solution is to simply wait, despite Paul's analyses.

C: André here; I'd like to comment on that. I'm not sure I agree with that, because as time passes the value decreases.

B: Well, in my opinion, that loss is not decreasing proportionately.

C: I really think it would be better to act now, Bert.

A: We've been arguing back and forth for some minutes now, and we're running short on time. However, we'll have to come to a consensus here, so I suggest we put it up for a vote now. Those of you in favour of the proposition please push the star key; all those opposed: please push the pound key. Thank you.

A: Ladies, gentlemen: on the screen I can now see the outcome of the vote, and the proposal has been adopted. It looks like we've run out of time, so I guess we'll have to adjourn our conference call here.

Cross-cultural negotiations

The next chapter is intended to raise your level of awareness of the many factors to consider when approaching an international negotiation. From experience, we advise you to develop a flexible personal negotiation style which will allow you to accommodate a variety of cultures. Before you make reservations to go to another country, invest some time acquainting yourself with the differences and similarities between you and the people on the other side of the conference table.

From the following pages you can learn more about:

- The relevance of focussing on relationship building (page 74),
- The consequences of sociolinguistic influences (page 75),
- The different expectations of negotiating processes across different cultures (page 80),
- Particular local negotiation techniques (page 83).

Relation orientation

Before engaging in negotiations, it may be helpful to look at the relevance of the focus of the negotiating partners. People, for instance, can be deal-focussed or relationship-focussed, and such a basic difference in focus can influence any negotiation. Additionally, age, gender, personality, or culture can also play a role. Some societies are more relationship-focussed. This means they prefer to build a relationship with the person, not the company or organisation. Trust is built up and any problems arising later can then be resolved personally. These societies rely less on written agreements, and you may expect lengthy, rapport-building preliminary small talk, before actually negotiating. Below is an overview of countries.

Deal-focussed	Moderately deal-focussed	Relationship-focussed
Germany	France	India
United States	Hungary	China
United Kingdom	Spain	Brazil
Sweden	Portugal	Emirates
Denmark	Italy	Japan
Australia	Hong Kong	Latin America
Switzerland	Singapore	Arab world
Netherlands	Poland	most of Asia
South Africa	Romania	most of Africa

Deal-focussed societies like the United States or Germany concentrate on the contract or written agreement and not so much on the relationship. When problems are encountered they return to the paperwork to clarify. The gap between such approaches is normally narrowed by a combination of relationship and deal-focussed orientation, but where the parties are both strictly adhering to their own approach, any deals reached are likely to unravel later. In the specific country chapters later on in this book, you will learn to deal with such differences in detail. This generally is necessary because contrasting values often cause conflict at the conference table.

Sociolinguistic influences

Interpreters at the European institutions in Brussels are only too aware of this: translating is also cultural enciphering. A word by word translation hardly represents the original intention of a text, because of the interlaced sociolinguistic influences. Is this of any consequence for negotiators? The answer is, that this is indeed plausible, looking at the examples of British English below.

Well-mannered

In Anglophone cultures, people are taught from childhood to use polite and indirect signals in their communication. And despite the different images that may exist about the British, Americans or say Australians, linguistic research has shown that all Anglo-Saxon cultures put strong emphasis on verbal politeness. German people don't interweave their phrases with the same number of "thank you's" and "please's", which is imperative for native English speakers. Therefore, just being able to translate German vocabulary into English, simply isn't enough. If the phrases below were translated into German literally, they might even be judged as too submissive:

- I was wondering if you could possibly reduce your initial offer to ...
- Excuse me, I was wondering whether I could copy your report?
- Do you think you could help me with that PowerPoint presentation?

English can be a rather formal language, which reflects its subtle sense of hierarchy. An easy memory aid for trying to be more polite is to simply use longer sentences. The three sample phrases above illustrate such different levels of indirectness also in phrase length.

Unspoken codes

There are various ways to express differences. Many of these are unspoken codes, or subtle distinctions that can be hard to distinguish for foreigners. The point is that in our upbringing we are often taught certain values. Cultural groups, for instance, the Germans, Swiss, Scandinavians or Dutch tend to be quite direct in their communication, and usually express exactly what they mean. Scientific research has shown that the way Germans express their thoughts can be quite to-the-point. The problem is that other cultures may sometimes perceive this to the point as just "blunt". Native English speakers tend to opt for highly scripted, requesting behaviour. The majority of the requests take the form of:

- Could you,
- Would you,
- Would you mind ~ing ...

Therefore try to be aware that the specific levels of directness appropriate for given situations might differ cross-culturally. And remember that a language like German tends to use more direct-level requests than British English. The table below shows a selection of cultures and their levels of directness in communication. The ranking of the United Kingdom explains the differences described above.

Switzerland (German-speaking)	More explicit communication
Germany	↓
Norway	
United States	
Netherlands	
Belgium (Flemish)	
France	
United Kingdom	
Italy	
Unit. Arab Emirates	
China	
Japan	More implicit communication

Levels of directness in speaking, by country

The table also makes clear why Americans generally use more direct and explicit communication. Indeed, British English can seem vague at times, but there's a very simple reason for that: vagueness is used to maintain politeness or avoid confrontation. The same applies to friendly small talk, humour and understatements, which are normally used to soften the style. Humour comes in many varieties in Britain, and can be used for all sorts of different situations: humour, self-mockery, criticism, paying a compliment, awkward moments, etc.

Non-verbal communication

International differences exist in the way people understand certain information. This may involve elements you don't always think of, like certain gestures you are used to making. A well known example is the OK sign (thumbs-up) and the perfect sign (thumb to forefinger, making a circle) because these can have offensive or insulting meanings in other cultures. The thumbs-up is comparable to raising the middle finger in large areas of Asia Minor, and the circle sign means "zéro" in France, money in Japan and the posterior opening of the alimentary canal in Brazil. Such unexpected differences can therefore cause misunderstandings. Like the typical Greek example of nodding which may be understood as a "Yes" where in fact it means "No". This is comparable in countries like Bulgaria, parts of Turkey, Iran and, for example, India. When doing business with someone from a different cultural background, it is worth researching this often forgotten element of communication beforehand.

Humour and jokes

Naturally cultural differences are reflected in our way of holding a meeting. In talks we will probably use some of the same strategies we are used to in face-to-face contact to ask or convince someone. The point is of course, that when we use a certain meeting style, this will influence the reaction of attendees at a meeting. This applies for the use of humour and jokes in a meeting. Anglophone negotiators make more and easier use of humour than for example German or Scandinavian speakers. A French or Russian speaker will probably prefer not to make any jokes, as that damages the desired image. Finding the correct type of humour is somewhat tricky, as humour doesn't always travel well. In Asian countries, types of humour like sarcasm, satire and parody aren't always understood or appreciated.

Useful vocabulary

submissive: unterwürfig
self-mockery: Selbstspott
posterior: Hintern
attendee: Anwesende

Using interpreters

It is of the highest importance to prepare interpreters and/or translators beforehand. This is done by means of small pre-talk and sending lists of jargon, key terms, common abbreviations and brand names. When negotiating with an interpreter, try to maintain eye contact with your negotiating counterpart, not with the interpreter. An interesting anecdote of how a senior Russian negotiator obtained an advantage in his negotiations with an American was his use of the interpreter. Despite the fact that the Russian spoke English adequately, he made use of an interpreter for an entirely different reason: while the interpreter was translating, the Russian could study the American's nonverbal expressions without hindrance. And when the American spoke, the Russian had twice the response time, because of the translation time required.

Negotiating internationally

Globalisation, not to mention the European single market, has been extending its influence on the way we work. As a consequence, we find ourselves having to communicate more and more with professionals from other countries. Recent research shows that international managers spend approximately twenty percent of their time on some sort of negotiation activity. Because negotiating is communicating to a large extent, it seems only logical that there will be local differences.

This book started by explaining many aspects of the English language but language constitutes only about thirty percent of overall communication. For that reason this section will now focus on other communication elements that play an essential role in international negotiating. Unfortunately, most books on international negotiating seem to revolve around the idea that there is one universal way of negotiating. This chapter tries to give you examples of how adapting elements of your usual negotiating tactics to particular cross-cultural differences will substantially improve your negotiation results.

Potential pitfalls

Techniques that work well at home, may fail in another country because the expectations of a negotiation party may simply be very different. The usual focus on win-win or win-lose cannot solve expectations in the fields of:

- Normal bargaining techniques,
- Terms for making convincing arguments,
- Expectations in regard to seniority,
- Ideas about hierarchy or decision-making authority,
- Habits in eye contact, interruption, intonation etc.
- Use of time.

A European study (Elucidate) clearly showed that around forty percent of the international negotiations in a European programme failed because of such cross-cultural conflicts. The problem is that most people who need to negotiate internationally haven't been schooled in this area. Usually only governments or large multinational corporations have specialists in that field. For most companies, negotiations abroad are carried out by those in middle management positions or technical specialists. So probably they will need to improvise, which in terms of risk management, can be problematic.

Different goals

Scientists interviewed negotiating teams from, amongst others, Japan, Brazil and the United States about their expectations for a specific negotiation. The analyses showed that culture does influence the expectation of a negotiation. The Japanese, for instance, were much more focussed on the long-term relations, whilst the Americans were mainly concerned about the short-term deal. The principal goal of the different negotiators also showed significant differences; where the Brazilian chief negotiator was concerned about achieving a respectable negotiation outcome, the Japanese negotiator was mainly focussed on market share, and the American on a short-term high profit. It is fair to say that some knowledge of specific Asian, Latin or western expectations will lead to better results.

Timing differs

What is the right moment to start the negotiating process? Do all cultures follow the same timing pattern as here in Germany? The answer is: absolutely not. People in neighbouring countries like France or Poland have different ideas on this. What, for instance, would be the right moment, to make an offer in France during a business lunch (dînatoire)? The answer is: probably close to the time dessert is being served. It is often felt that starting business any earlier could be too blunt. The overview below shows us which selected trade cultures open talks directly, and which cultures use more small talk, because they consider it less well-mannered starting straight away:

Country	Early	Half	Late
Germany	✓		
China			✓
Emirates			✓
Finland	✓		
France			✓
Italy			✓
Japan			✓
Netherlands	✓		
Poland		✓	
Portugal			✓
Spain			✓
Sweden	✓		
United Kingdom		✓	
United States	✓		

Local negotiation techniques

Scientists have studied negotiation techniques in Japan, Brazil and the United States in combined research of universities from the same countries. They interviewed various participants and analysed many hours of video recordings. The results showed some remarkable differences.

Behaviour tactics	Japan	US	Brazil
Silent Periods (number of silent periods longer than 10 seconds, per 30 minutes)	5.5	2.5	0
Overlaps (number per 10 min)	12.6	10.3	28.6

Behaviour tactics	Japan	US	Brazil
Facial Looking (minutes of gazing per 10 min)	1.3	3.3	5.2
Touching (per 30 min / not including handshaking)	0	0	4.7

The Japanese, for instance, can maintain several seconds of total silence. When a negotiator isn't aware of this, he or she may be influenced by a silence that means something other than expected. In Mediterranean cultures on the contrary, people can overlap in their conversation, meaning that people talk simultaneously. The same applies for interrupting people. This is considered rude in north-western European cultures, but in more southern cultures it is quite normal, and as such, thought of as a form of active listening. The table above also shows us that Brazilian negotiators touch their counterparts much more. The so-called comfort zone between people in Brazil is also much smaller than, for instance, in Germany. Latin people feel, especially when talking about confidential matters, that they want to stand closer to each other. Northern people, however, usually feel uncomfortable and try to create some space, often by stepping back a bit. It can sometimes lead to amusing movement patterns of participants at international summits.

Compromises

Making a compromise is considered positive in certain cultures and in other cultures not. For instance, the Dutch, Belgians or Swedes have learned to compromise from a young age on, whereas Russians, Spaniards or French have developed skills in another direction. A Spaniard, for example, generally believes that a compromise might damage his honour (pundonor). Knowledge of such cultural differences can help in preparing appropriately, and should assist in negotiating more successfully.

Look me in the eyes

As the table above shows, the time spent looking directly into each other eyes makes up only thirteen percent of the time in a country like Japan. Indeed in Asian cultures direct eye contact is generally seen as assertive or emphatic. Many people in the West wouldn't trust someone who avoids eye contact of one form or another, and people in the Middle-East use much stronger eye contact in negotiations than Europeans.

Listening habits

The way you prepare for a negotiation should take into account which opponent you are addressing. Research shows that the way specific cultures talk and listen differs to a great extent. An example: German, Swedish, Dutch and Finnish business cultures put great emphasis on factual information and they know how to listen well. Spaniards, French or Italians, according to their expectations, prefer imaginative topics. They prefer using eloquent phrases and knowing how to present themselves. They would much rather hear things presented with flair or grandeur than dry facts or technical details. The same applies for the listening span, which can be relatively short.

Strategic negotiating framework

Stephen Weiss examined cultural aspects of the international negotiating process. He concluded after studying many negotiation cases, that for successful outcomes it mattered that negotiators reflect on their own cultural negotiation script, as well as on that of the other parties involved. By choosing strategies accordingly better results were achieved. Depending on how much knowledge each party had of the culture of the other party, a choice for a negotiation sequence or script could be made. Depending on the scale of such awareness one of four possible scripts can be elected for a maximal international negotiating outcome.

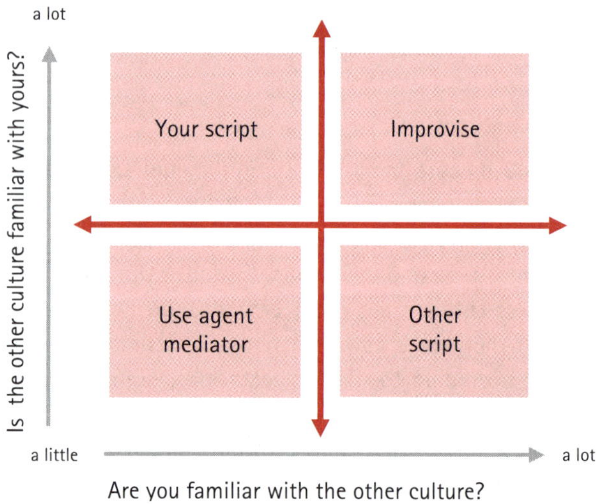

The four options of the Weiss framework

Country-specific negotiating

National culture is one of the factors that influence behaviour at the negotiation table, just like personality, gender or organisational culture. But recent scientific research has shown that there are considerable differences in approach, and perhaps that explains why forty percent of international negotiations seem to fail. In this chapter you will gain insight for selected trade cultures into the following aspects of negotiating:

- Country typical meeting behaviour (page 89),
- Relevant local value systems (page 112).

Introduction

This part of the book is dedicated to specific communication habits and local value differences per country. And as the world seems to be getting smaller and smaller, the chances of negotiating with partners from less familiar cultures are augmenting strongly. Such negotiations often take place in English, but because language only counts for some thirty percent of communication, it is helpful to have some insight into the other elements that influence the way people communicate in a particular country. Since the eighties of the last century more and more research has been published on comparing national negotiation styles. Trainers, consultants, as well as Chambers of Commerce offer all sorts of seminars to help businessmen prepare for negotiating with foreign opponents. It seems there is a practical need. And since negotiating relies so strongly on communication, a fair amount of it will relate to cross-cultural awareness.

With the use of internet technology nowadays there are some very useful tools available in order to compare the average values or rankings of countries. Partly based on world wide surveys, partly based on statistics, such information may help to predict behaviour. Even as a generalisation (as no human being can be put on a list), this predictability is helpful for developing a negotiations strategy for a foreign country. The next pages introduce such country-specific behaviour for the (weighted) main trade partners of Germany.

China

Despite the fact that the word "foreigner" translates as "yang guizi" (foreign devil) in Mandarin, China is Germany's eighth export market, and its second biggest import partner (after the Netherlands). Looking at the economic forecasts, the export of goods will increase substantially in all likelihood. When dealing with Chinese take the following aspects into account.

Meeting

Preliminary meetings mainly serve to get to know each other better, business therefore isn't really discussed. The Chinese speak less, and use longer periods of total silence (in China silence is also eloquence). The Chinese language also knows many different wording possibilities depending on the status of someone. This calls for skilled interpreters or translators. Individual expression of thought is less common in China, as it may harm consensus. Creative brainstorming during a meeting will not produce many results; it will be more effective to adjourn, allowing your Chinese opponent room for thinking. There are usually (hard working) note takers present at meetings to produce detailed minutes. Chinese feel less ruled by their agenda.

Negotiations

It is interesting to see how Chinese make deals, as they tend to think much more about the consequences of a deal for their relationship networks. Preparation therefore usually includes collecting data on people and the involved relations (guanxi). Important business decisions tend to take a long time, due to the desire for consensus. Foreign parties negotiating mainly need patience, and that's something the Chinese have plenty of. Government approval is indispensable (national, local, as well as provincial) for any major project. This influences both planning as well as profits sometimes. Contracts are considered less binding than in western trade cultures.

Relevant values

Confucian values still influence the Chinese society to a large extent. As common in collectivist cultures, the stronger party is generally expected to accommodate the weaker party. This underlying value also applies to negotiations sometimes. Protocol and hierarchy are omnipotent. Chinese schools, for instance, are used to very strict discipline. Corruption is not uncommon. Statistics show that Germans are three times more individual than the Chinese, and only half as hierarchically orientated. For a complete overview of all variable scores and rankings, please refer to the tables on pages 105 and 106 of this book. Some influential values or patterns are described below:

- It's not what you know, but who you know ("guanxi"),
- Seniority and connections cancel out achievements,
- Behave harmoniously and show respect to authority,
- It's impolite to say "no" or openly criticise (loss of face),
- Only do so in private with close ones ("naixin"),
- Do not directly display negative emotions.

Czech Republic

The Czech Republic represents the westernmost presence of Slavic culture in Europe. It is a stable environment for foreign trade and business investment opportunities, given the fact that nowadays foreign-owned companies account for seventy percent of its exports. The chances of having to negotiate with a Czech opponent are considerable, as thirty percent of all foreign trade is conducted with Germany. When dealing with Czech counterparts take the following aspects into account.

Meeting

As is the case in German business life, Czechs prefer to plan meetings in advance. Points on an agenda are to be followed; people are good listeners and do not really interrupt each other. During meetings, the Czech shows calmness and self-control. A display of emotions is less likely than in neighbouring countries such as Poland or Hungary. As a result the (measured) tone of voice is usually softer. Discussions proceed in an orderly fashion and decision-making is usually methodical.

Negotiations

Just like Germans, the Czechs are task-oriented, meaning that very little time is spent on small talk at the beginning of negotiations. Besides, the Czechs are known for a very direct communication style, again like in Germany. The only difference is that they can be less straightforward when saying "No", and might feel less comfortable giving negative answers. Argumentation is best done with empirical evidence and facts supporting the proposals. Step-by-step consensus seeking techniques give better results than aggressive negotiation tactics. Czechs aren't very fond of arguing or haggling; therefore it is advisable to keep the difference between the starting price and the final price within a logical margin. Business meals play less of a role, as Czechs separate business and social circles.

Relevant values

The Czechs have a tradition of avoiding conflict and confrontation, as the Czech national history proves. Take, for instance, the "Velvet Revolution" of 1989 which took place without violence as did the "Velvet Divorce" of 1993, when Czechoslovakia peacefully split into the Czech and the Slovak Republic. The values scores aren't very different, except for the hierarchical acceptance, which is almost double that of the German score. Other significant differences are the amount of bureaucracy and the relatively higher corruption perception index. For a complete overview of all variable scores and rankings, please refer to the tables on pages 105 and 106 of this book.

> Command of languages in the Czech Republic:
> German: 28%, English: 24%, Russian: 20%.

Useful vocabulary

task-oriented: aufgabenorientiert
straightforward: geradeheraus, unkompliziert
haggle: herunterhandeln, feilschen

France

France has been Germany's number one export partner for many years now, and those who have dealt professionally with "la douce France" know how different business communication can be. Some relevant differences are described below.

Meeting

The French are trained in both debating skills as well as analysis from an early age. It is generally considered important to prove a point by way of logical argumentation. The simple notion that the facts are different is not always accepted, if not backed up by lengthy rhetorical argumentation. Meetings are not always grounds for discussion, but are often used to inform about what has been decided. Business lunches may last two hours. Don't let business be a topic of conversation too early, and therefore prepare something else to talk about.

Negotiations

The French can be persistent at times when a strategy has been chosen. Compromise isn't considered a very positive thing by everyone. A direct "No" is (unlike in Germany) generally avoided. The French prefer to say something like: "Oui mais" (yes, but), "Oui-non, nous verrons" (yes-no, we'll see) or even "Si vous voulez" (if you like). It is a mistake not to understand such remarks as a "Non". Whatever is being proposed or agreed upon during negotiations, will only be a sure thing when approved afterwards by the PDG (Président Directeur Général).

Relevant values

Most value scores are comparable to the German ones. However, hierarchical acceptance is twice as strong as in Germany, as is the corruption perception. For a complete overview of all variable scores and rankings, please refer to the tables on pages 105 and 106 of this book.

- In France some forty percent of higher functions are occupied by women,
- Using beautiful language combined with semi-philosophical logic seems to be a goal in itself,
- Etiquette is a French word, and knowledge thereof may give some self-assurance,
- Being refined or special is an important quality that is reflected in the choice of negotiation venue, restaurant, wines, as well as clothing.

> Command of languages in France:
> English: 36%, Spanish: 13%, German: 8%.

Useful vocabulary

obstinately: stur
self-assurance: Selbstbewusstsein
venue: Handlungsort
command of languages: Sprachkenntnisse

India

The second most populated country of the world is at present Germany's twenty-fifth trade partner. In the near future, however, India will play a more prominent role in global economics. First of all the population is growing faster than China's and the GDP is also increasing rapidly. Today India has about three hundred million middle class consumers, but the country adds a North Rhine-Westphalia every single year (...).

Meeting

Indians have a preference for eloquent respectful speakers. Too many dry facts don't work well. Meetings will contain a semi-euphoric atmosphere with sympathetic verbose talks in Victorian English. Despite the fact that certain Hindi words have become part of (financial) Indian English, it is advisable to study the most common of these beforehand. Many meetings will not follow an agenda, will have plenty of interruptions, and may possibly go over time. Therefore, don't make too many appointments on one day, and take the dense traffic into consideration as well.

Negotiations

Negotiations normally start in a sympathetic atmosphere, whilst the negotiation part can be serious with long haggling. Expect negotiations to be long, but usually changes will be proposed in a polite way to find agreement. The ease of doing business ranking, as well as legal contract enforcing possibilities is low compared to European standards. Insert mediation and arbitration clauses in all legal contracts. Be careful that Indians cannot directly say "No", and will therefore normally revert to expressions like: "maybe", "we'll try" and so forth. Vice versa, Germans should be careful with saying "No" too directly. Decisions need to be ratified by the higher levels; therefore check already during negotiations which parts have been firmly agreed and which not. Socialising can be a pleasant part of business in India, and Indian hospitality has a lot to offer visitors. On the other hand, I know that Indians visiting North-West Europe can be surprised or disappointed with the treatment given.

Relevant values

India is a contact instead of a contract culture, where relationships are more important than a deal at hand. Companies are strictly hierarchical and empowerment is hardly seen, although a younger generation is getting a taste of it at universities now.

- Getting frustrated will neither help, nor win friends,
- Value is placed on empathy and consensus,
- Dinners start late and last long.

Useful vocabulary

verbosity: Wortschwall
dense: zusammengedrängt
mediation: Vermittlung
revert to: zurückgreifen auf

Italy

Italian culture has had a demonstrable influence: the Roman Empire, the Renaissance or the weight of the Vatican. As a country, Germany is Italy's main trading partner, both in import and export. Most of the Italian businesses are SMEs (KMU), almost three-quarters of the Italian economy in tact. Moreover, quite a few of these are family run businesses. It is plausible that this might affect negotiations in some way.

Meeting

Initial meetings in Italy are usually intended to get people acquainted, not to do straight business. Meetings themselves often seem noisy and unstructured compared to German standards. There is a considerably longer time frame reserved for small talk, and mobile phone calls are often acceptable during a meeting. Improvisation is valued, just as interruptions, and indeed many Italians think that following the agenda strictly could interfere with the quality of a discussion. Italians also prefer to present an argument in an articulate way, partly because "feeling" is recognised as a factor in decision making.

> Command of languages in Italy:
> English: 29%, French: 14%.

Negotiations

Negotiating in Italy can sometimes be a lengthy process, where patience works much better than irritation, because business and social life can be so intermingled. Personal alliances are often influential in Italy. It's not "what" you know, but "who" you know, and people are also judged on their ability to cultivate relationships. Smaller companies tend to have a rather hierarchical structure, often with an autocratic style of management. In Germany, the facts are much more separated from the person; Italians tend to take direct rejections more personally. They also may feel that Germans are overly concerned with facts and procedures and like to explore a contextual background. Perhaps they feel that the over-pragmatic Northerners lack a sense of deeper thinking.

Relevant values

Jokes and private remarks are exchanged much more than in Germany, and are judged as functional in a business environment. Italians have difficulty saying "No" directly.

- Successful business relations invest in socialising,
- Pay attention to dress and style, as often someone is judged on that,
- "La bella figura" refers to more than just fashion; charm, formal elegance, tact and confidence also play an important role in Italy,
- Italian contracts can be written in a labyrinthine way and contain complicated terminology,

Useful vocabulary

SME (small and medium enterprises, USA: SMB): KMU (kleine und mittlere Unternehmen)
interfere with: beeinträchtigen

Japan

Although its economy has stagnated recently, Japan is still one of the world's richest societies – with one and a half times as many inhabitants as Germany, and Greater Tokyo as the largest metropolitan area in the world, with over 30 million residents.

Meeting

Initial meetings in Japan are intended to get people acquainted, and reinforce a consensus that may already have been established. They do not serve to do straight business. The atmosphere in Japanese meetings tends to be highly formal (in contrast to the business entertaining afterwards). Japanese negotiators generally like to be well informed about the focus of a meeting and who will be attending, so they can prepare a well-matched team. Be clear about the status of the members in the organisation (also on business cards). Some communication distinctions influence Japanese business meetings compared to elsewhere. This primarily has to do with:

- Difficulties due to English language abilities,
- The particular importance of inexplicit and polite conversational style, (never interrupt, apologize non-stop),
- The long silences in between phrases.

Negotiations

Negotiating in Japan can be a lengthy process, where patience is a necessary commodity. This is because teams never make decisions at the meeting. The main reason is that a consensus has to be reached within the own company departments, as well as with other existing relationships. Japanese negotiation teams give the least information compared to other cultures, whereas German negotiation teams score highest. On the other hand, the Japanese are willing to make the most concessions, while the Germans are the toughest negotiators. In Japan, the customer and supplier relationship shows a very different power balance than is customary in Germany, where the customer does not play as strong a role. The Japanese value long-term relationships.

Relevant values

Japanese businesses prefer to first establish the right relationships before business can be conducted. After this, people work in a quite task-oriented manner and with self-effacing dedication. The Japanese expect people to show self-knowledge of their position and behave accordingly; therefore, what is not said can also be very important.

- The Japanese tend to be inconceivably conscious of detail,
- "Saving face" is essential in interpersonal contact,
- Japan's corruption index is comparable to Germany's,
- The Japanese have one of the highest scores on status.

Useful vocabulary

commodity: Handelsartikel
self-effacing: zurückhaltend
inconceivably: unfassbar

Netherlands

This small neighbouring country has the highest density in Europe (one fifth of the German population, living on one tenth of its area). And it may come as a surprise that the Netherlands have become Germany's number one trade partner. .On the other hand, the Dutch focus has been on Germany for many years, with more than two-thirds of its population speaking (some) German.

Meeting

Dutch meetings are pragmatic and quickly focus on results and responsibilities with clear action plans. During meetings, everybody may contribute and voice an opinion, whether it is positive or negative. The goal of meetings is consensus-building and planning. The Dutch are used to freedom and assertiveness starting from a young age and they communicate accordingly. They are quicker on first-name terms and seem less driven by protocol. The Dutch value experiment, and don't mind making tentative suggestions during meetings.

> Command of languages in the Netherlands:
> English: 87%, German: 70%, French: 29%, Spanish: 11%.

Negotiations

Negotiators tend to get right down to business, with little time for small talk or getting acquainted. Dutch can be direct in asking what they are looking for. Despite well-defined divisions of tasks, the Dutch are used to speaking up openly in negotiations. And although time efficiency is usually a leitmotif, the decision-making process may take time because of the need for in-company consensus.

Relevant values

The Dutch society is characterized by open-mindedness and tolerance. It is also remarkably egalitarian, with flat and transparent management structures. The biggest value differences between the Netherlands and Germany is the lower Dutch score on achievement orientation, and the stronger position of women in society.

- Dutch can be more pragmatic and as such, deviate from fixed procedures,
- To discuss business details during lunch or dinner is quite normal,
- Socialising mainly happens after a good working relationship has been established between parties,
- Too open displays of wealth are generally distrusted, partly due to their (mainly) Calvinistic background,
- Dutch are allowed to make jokes, while being serious.

Useful vocabulary

density: Dichte
assertiveness: Durchsetzungsfähigkeit
accordingly: dementsprechend
division of tasks: Aufgabenverteilung
deviate from: abweichen von

Poland

Poland constitutes the largest market in Central Europe; from the Polish perspective Germany is the largest trade partner.

Meeting

Meetings in Poland start and finish relatively on time and few interruptions occur. Poles do not always prepare for meetings, since they also have a social function. Poles prefer a face-to-face meeting over an e-mail. This proves that despite the fact every culture uses the same means of communication, the difference often occurs in how and when the media are deployed. Initial meetings in Poland, for instance, are often just opportunities for establishing relationships, not making business decisions. Socialising after work is very common and a necessary aspect of gaining trust. Meetings can start earlier, due to the Polish daily schedule, which starts and finishes earlier.

Command of languages in Poland:
English: 29%, Russian: 26%, German: 19%.

Negotiations

The fact that the Poles use the word "rozmowy" (conversation) more than the word "negocjacje" (negotiation), indicates the importance of enough warming-up time in developing business relationships. In German business life, people are used to strict planning, detailed discussions and a separation between their private and professional lives – three things that are quite different when doing business in Poland. Poles value improvising skills more; therefore general task descriptions or milestones have proven to be more acceptable. In addition, negotiations may take more time; therefore only the patient managers manage in Poland.

Relevant values

Generally speaking, Polish business culture has been characterised as one with a hands-on mentality mixed with emotional decision-making. Foreign managers initially seem unaware of the patience and understanding required for the local differences. If we look at the style of communication, Poles tend to express themselves in a formal but more indirect way than Germans, and prefer expressive capacity and anecdotes or metaphors over literal messages. On the other hand, people can ask explicitly for information or when making requests. But generally they don't like to say "No" ("nie") directly, and likewise, they also don't like to be told "No".

- Leadership uses hierarchy to a large extent,
- The Catholic religion is a powerful value in Poland,
- The level and influence of bureaucracy are still apparent, although not always transparent.

Useful vocabulary

constitute: darstellen
deploy: einsetzen
hands-on: praktisch
apparent: wahrnehmbar

Russia

Russia is the world's largest country in size, and about fifty times as big as Germany. The Russian economy is connecting more and more with the European Union and hence the number of professional contacts is also increasing. Visiting negotiators find that the Russian business culture has its own characteristics, as described below:

Meeting

Russians tend to care less for punctuality, as meetings do not only start later, but also run longer than anticipated. Interruptions and conversations on the side are frequent, and the agenda is not always adhered to. Russians are generally well educated and like ornamental metaphors or story-telling in business. Therefore an exposé full of facts will not challenge their minds. Meetings in Russia are not always result-focused, while much time may be devoted to discussing and understanding a problem. This may challenge the minds of German managers. In Russia, meetings might end with the signing of a protocol, which is simply a report of what was said but has no legal implication.

Negotiations

As in many countries, a senior negotiation team will receive more respect, regardless of the decision-making authority. Russians in general negotiate to win, not to find a consensus. It is wise to slot in enough room for negotiations or trade offs. Just as in chess games, negotiators will think several moves ahead. Vodka toasting is a symbolic element in Russian business entertainment, and may happen directly after an agreement. A contract is often considered less binding than it is here, and in many companies unanimity is prescribed for essential choices.

Relevant values

Russians have a strong sense of national pride for "Motherland" (родин, rodina). Unlike in Germany, planning is not seen as omnipotent, and work and private life will be quite mixed. Just as in Asia, the so-called "loss of face" is an important value. It is important to use the word "No" carefully, or give direct criticism or complaints. Business can still be rather bureaucratic, and to obtain faster results in Russia, the use of personal networks (блат, blat) can be indispensable.

- Power is very centralised and often concentrated,
- Status is an important aspect of Russian society,
- A person who only concentrates on business, might come across as less trustful,
- Instead of dry facts, intellectual and philosophical debate is higher valued,
- The working day may start quite early.

Useful vocabulary

to adhere: erfüllen, einhalten
trade off: Austausch
indispensable: unentbehrlich
exposé: Bericht
omnipotent: allmächtig

Spain

The country Spain is about one and a half times the size of Germany, and more than half of the German population.Business in Spain is usually acquired through personal relationships; therefore business entertaining is an essential pro-cess of any professional contact. The substantial differences in conducting meetings and negotiations are explained below:

Meeting

Initial meetings in Spain are usually just meant for becoming acquainted, not to do straight business. Meetings are different compared to German standards, as they often don't follow an agenda order, and people frequently interrupt each other (which isn't judged negatively). Agendas play a lesser role, because meetings serve more to exchange ideas and to invest in the personal relationships, than actually reaching decisions. Meetings also often run over time. On the other hand, a Spaniard doesn't say that "time flies", but that "time walks". And indeed the word "mañana" can refer to a moment in time, not necessarily being tomorrow. The siesta interruption was abolished by the Spanish government in 2005, although certain companies might have a separate morning or (late) afternoon staff.

Negotiations

Hierarchical acceptance in Spain is double that of what it is in Germany, and indeed Spanish leadership is characterised by both its charismatic and autocratic aspects. In order to successfully negotiate with Spaniards, it is also essential to realise that the need for facts and planning isn't supported in the same way in Spain. Spanish negotiations often follow the win-lose concept. Therefore preparations should focus on negotiable points and parrying bargaining. Spaniards are also articulate and meandering speakers, connecting to the larger picture, perhaps even philosophical concepts. As they are relationship and not task-orientated, a fair amount of socialising will probably take place after negotiation rounds.

Relevant values

- Face-to-face contact is preferred over e-mail or phone.
- Wait long enough before talking business at business lunches, or let your Spanish counterpart lead.
- To openly damage someone's pride is a cardinal sin.
- There are very strong regional sentiments, with their own language and identity.
- Most people speak "castellano" as the term "español" usually denotes federal things.
- Spain has an enormous number of public holidays.

Useful vocabulary

abolish: abschaffen
parry: parieren, abwehren
meandering: mäandern, abschweifen

United Kingdom

The United Kingdom comprises Great Britain and Northern Ireland. And although described as incurably insular and different, Britons are nevertheless Germany's fifth trading partner. Those who conduct meetings and negotiations with British people often describe them as different from those on the continent. The following paragraph takes a closer look:

Meeting

Meetings in Britain typically begin and end with small talk. Meetings will be structured, but perhaps less so than one is used to at home. During the course of the meeting it is acceptable for people to take calls, or join later (or walk out earlier). In addition, people will not always have spent a lot of time preparing for a meeting. Discussion is an essential part of meetings, as is debating, but the British don't appreciate open verbal conflict. Their communication style uses politeness as a courtesy. Not only do British managers use their sense of humour in business meetings, they also have a great many varieties: irony, sarcasm, self-mockery etc., and these are generally called for with professional purposes in mind.

Negotiations

When preparing negotiations, it is useful to know that British managers prefer target-driven proposals that yield short-term benefits. A non-disclosure agreement is quite common, and shouldn't really be seen as distrust. Negotiators are often empowered to make decisions and get things done; most

British firms nowadays have an increasingly flat hierarchical structure. After the initial meeting, first names are quickly used; academic credentials don't play much of role. After-work drinking is quite a common thing. British negotiators can be rather vague when declining an idea or proposal. This indirectness is referred to as "coded speech". An example is when someone doesn't agree and she/he will say: "hmm, that's an interesting idea". It might help to study facial expressions closely or the tone of voice for that matter. Command of foreign languages is limited in the populated south part of Britain.

Relevant values

British managers look for a leadership style in which they will seem reasonable and righteous. Although British value scores hardly differ from German ones, British culture has a higher degree of individualism. In fact, it is the only language which capitalises the word "I".

- One should never make a scene,
- The British typically have a sense of fair play,
- The class system is still evident in Britain.

Useful vocabulary

insular: insular, inselartig
take a call: einen Anruf entgegennehmen
self-mockery: Selbstspott
decline: ablehnen
tone of voice: Tonfall
righteous: rechtschaffen

United States

Knowing the United States through popular culture (for instance cinema), isn't the same as doing business with Americans. The following paragraphs inform you in brief about the cultural business norms of the United States of America, a country spanning six times zones.

Meeting

Meetings generally are seen as a platform to make decisions and drive action by the end of the meeting. Most Americans tend to have a preference for incomplex empirical information, adhering to the KISS axiom (keep it short and simple). They are quick to use first names or even nicknames, and do not care for academic credentials. As most professionals are very busy, meetings can take place over business breakfasts or after work. The focus on time management is very strong in the United States.

Negotiations

Negotiating in the States is often characterised by so-called "hard sell". American negotiators prefer to secure a favourable deal or short-term commercial results. They do so in an informal way, using a direct assertive communication style and logical reasoning for the most part. Self-promotion is judged positively, because a confident strong pitch creates trust. Americans negotiators expect decisions to be taken during a negotiation, and are usually empowered to agree, without approval of senior leadership. In wanting to secure an agreement, some negotiators may "take no for an answer". Americans generally prefer target-driven proposals that yield short-term benefits. Convincing arguments will focus primarily on speed, cost and efficiency. Although information is shared openly between partners, information may be released in negotiations only after signing a non-disclosure agreement. Contracts and legal documents tend to be very lengthy in the US.

Relevant values

The cultural value scores aren't that different from the German ones, expect that Americans are highly individualistic; in fact English is the only language which capitalises the word "I".

- America is a can-do, achievement-focused culture,
- Americans might prepare less than Germans in advance,
- There is a high tolerance for failure in the US.

Useful vocabulary

axiom: Grundsatz
credential: Diplom
pitch: Verkaufsmasche
non-disclosure agreement: Vertraulichkeitsvereinbarung

Cross-cultural differences

The table on the following pages quantifies the relevant cross-cultural differences in the field of international negotiating for the selected countries. The following seven indicators have been used:

1 Population/area (compared to Germany),
2 German trade rank (weighted export/import),
3 Ease of doing business,
4 Enforcing contracts,
5 Corruption perception,
6 Achievement orientation,
7 Hierarchical orientation,
8 Individualism.

Figures under number one show how many times a country and its population is smaller or bigger than Germany. The values of the numbers two to four are ranking indicators, of which the "Ease of doing business" and the "Enforcing contracts" come from the yearly country ranking of the World Bank (183 countries in total). The first indicator is based on the study of laws and regulations which influence doing business in a country. Thus, if a country has a low ranking, it is logical to expect influences on the time line of a negotiation, and a delay doesn't necessarily have to mean tactics of the negotiating partner. The indicator "Corruption perception" is a yearly index of transparency.org (180 countries). These three mentioned rankings are weighted in order to offer you a more long-term view. For this table, the average from 2004 to 2008 is taken and added to the 2009 score. Where possible or applicable, future forecasts of the Economist Intelligence Unit have been used for rounding off an amount to the nearest decimal.

The indicator numbers six to eight are at a country level and unchangeable. The three indices used are: "Achievement orientation", "Hierarchical acceptance", and "Individualism". They refer to the country scores of the cultural dimensions research by Geert Hofstede. In his (original) study, scores from 1 to 100 were possible. For example, the German 35 score for hierarchical acceptance (originally called: PDI or power distance index) is much lower than the Chinese score of 80, but more than double the Austrian score of 14. We can also see that the average German score is much higher than the Chinese score as far as individualism is concerned. Such statistics may help to predict behaviour and think of a strategy when preparing for negotiations. For example, in the case of China, the power of a decision of a negotiating partner may be limited by hierarchical approval, whereas a German export manager may have more possibilities to make decisions on the spot. This means that negotiations might take longer, which in turn has an influence on the planning of a business trip and the number of possible appointments.

Another interesting aspect is that research shows that in countries with a high hierarchical acceptance score, the value of written contracts is considered lower than the opinion of the highest management.

In short: although this table presents a great many combinations of dry numbers, it does in fact offer the reader a chance to forecast negotiating positions driven by culture.

Countries: Statistics and value facts

Country	Population/ area (in times Germany)	German trade rank export/ import	Ease of doing business	Enforcing contracts
Germany			25	7
China	16,3 27	8 2	89	18
Czech Republic	0,1 0,2	12 10	74	82
France	0,8 1,8	1 3	31	6
India	14,4 9	12 10	133	182
Italy	0,7 0,8	5 5	78	156
Japan	1,6 1,1	18 14	15	20
Nether- lands	0,2 0,1	2 1	30	30
Poland	0,5 0,9	10 12	72	75
Russia	1,7 48	13 11	120	19
Spain	0,6 1,4	11 13	62	52
UK	0,8 0,7	4 6	5	23
USA	3,8 27	3 4	4	8

Country	Corruption perception	Achievement orientation	Hierarchy orientation	Indivi-dualism
Germany	14	66	35	67
China	80	66	80	20
Czech Republic	52	57	57	58
France	24	43	68	71
India	84	56	77	48
Italy	63	70	50	76
Japan	17	95	54	46
Nether-lands	6	14	38	80
Poland	51	64	68	60
Russia	149	36	93	39
Spain	33	42	57	51
UK	18	66	35	89
USA	19	62	40	91

Practical reference

Financial numbers

When writing numbers or amounts of money, the English language observes a few other conventions compared to German. The most important difference probably is the reverse use of commas and full stops (periods). Australian texts may use a space instead of a comma, and Swiss texts often use an apostrophe to separate the thousands. The position of the currency can be placed before or behind the amount, depending on the local linguistic convention. There is no space between the British pound sign and the amount in English, unlike the German habit.

Is this important in negotiations? An answer to that question may be best given by the mistake of aeronautics company Lockheed Martin. as they lost seventy million dollars, when they agreed to an equation for adjusting the sales price for changes to the inflation rate. The reason: because of the difference between periods and commas...

Decimal points

The examples below show you how to pronounce numbers with decimal points in them, as well as amounts of money and temperatures:

Number	Pronouncing
3.50	three point five oh
45	forty-five
550	five hundred and fifty

Number	Pronouncing
6 500	six thousand five hundred, or: sixty-five hundred
75 000	seventy-five thousand
850 000	eight hundred and fifty thousand
9 500 000	nine million five hundred thousand, or: nine and a half million
-5.9	minus five point nine
-20 000	minus twenty thousand
10 °C	ten degrees Celsius, or: ten degrees centigrade

Indicating larger numbers

For describing larger amounts or numbers in the English language you may come across the following abbreviations:

- thousand: K
- million: m
- billion (in German: Milliarde): bn
- trillion (in German: Billion): T
- quadrillon (in German: Billiarde)

A billion is a thousand million, a trillion a thousand billion, a quadrillion a thousand trillion. Monetary units, such as dollars or pound sterling, are often abbreviated with their own currency symbols. Note that in the United Kingdom a middle dot is often used as the decimal point on price stickers (e.g.: £6·95). Besides the currency symbols, you may also wish to use the international monetary abbreviations as stated in the list of currencies from the International Organization for Standardization (ISO 4217: Currency names and code elements). Then the word "euro" is written in small letters in English. EU legislation prescribes the use of the words "euro" and "cent" in both singular and plural. But in the rest of the English-speaking world it is common to use the natural plural in -s. Most financial media in the UK also prefer "euros" and "cents" in the plural form.

Fractions

Generally fractions are used for rough figures (e.g.: a hectare is 2½ acres) and decimals for more exact figures (although in reality fractions are more precise than decimals). Do note the hyphen between the elements of a fraction, for instance: three-quarters. Further, the preposition "of" is used when describing fractions. For example: two-fifths of our clients. Just less than two-thirds of our customers.

Symbol	Word
1/2	a half, half, one-half
1/3	a third, one-third
2/3	two-thirds
1/4	one-quarter
3/4	three-quarters three fourths (us)
1/5	one-fifth
5/6	five-sixths
1/8	one-eighth
3/8	three-eighths
10/10	ten out of ten

Language transfer

Language transfer means that a speaker applies elements from his native language to a foreign language. This could be grammar influences, but the most common form of language transfer is known as "false friends". It is interesting that psychologists have reported that when people speak English as a second language, the tendency is to use the English word but retain its primary language's meaning for that word. The table below contains pairs of words that look similar, but differ in meaning in two languages. Because false friends are a problem for second-language speakers, the table below compiles both German-English as well as English-German false friends.

English	German	False friend	Translation
to get	bekommen	to become	werden
management	Direktion	direction	Richtung
competition	Konkurrenz	concurrence	Übereinkunft
draft, plan	Konzept	concept	Begriff, Idee
corporate	Konzern	concern	Belang
CEO	Manager	manager	Filialleiter
brand	Marke	mark	Note
fair; mass	Messe	mess	Unordnung
personnel	Personal	personal	persönlich
entrepreneur	Unternehmer	undertaker	Leichenbestatter
if	wenn	when	wann

Identical words too abstract

The English language knows some words that are identical to German words. The problem is that we tend to use such words a lot, as they are frequently used in German, but that they can sound rather abstract in English. To avoid such stylistic pitfalls it is sometimes better to use other alternatives. The table below gives an overview.

English	German	Alternative
initiative	Initiative	proposal
integral	integral	entire, total
optimal	optimal	ideal
philosophy	Philosophie	approach
realise	realisieren	achieve
vision	Vision	view
perspective	Perspektive	expectation

British and American English

There are some differences in spelling or vocabulary, although not many words cause misunderstandings. A relevant example for negotiations is the expression "to table a motion". Which in the UK means: "to place it on the agenda", while in the US this means exactly the opposite: "to remove it from consideration". No idea how this is dealt with in bilateral negotiations... George Bernard Shaw once wrote: "Britain and America are two countries divided by a common language". That probably sounds a bit tall; nevertheless, really different words are sometimes used. Some of the more common ones are mentioned in the table below (listed by German translation, for convenience):

British English	American English	German
at cost price	at cost	Selbstkostenpreis
autumn	fall	Herbst
banking account	bank account	Bankkonto
banknote	bill	Banknote
bill	check	Rechnung
booking	reservation	Reservierung
company	corporation	Betrieb
enquiry	inquiry	Erkundigung
expiry date	expiration date	Verfallsdatum
inland revenue	duty income tax	Steuereinnahmen
let	hire	vermieten
solicitor/barrister	attorney	Rechtsanwalt
transport	transportation	Transport

Delivery and Incoterms

The Incoterms 2000 (International Commercial Terms: Internationale Handelsklauseln) are a series of international sales terms which serve to divide transaction costs and responsibilities between buyer and seller. They are usually mentioned in an abbreviation + city combination (e.g.: our prices are FOB Hamburg).

Abbrevia-tion	English	German
Group E		
EXW	Ex Works	Ab Werk
Group F		
FCA	Free Carrier	Frei Frachtführer
FAS	Free Alongside Ship	Frei Längsseite Schiff
FOB	Free On Board	Frei an Bord
Group C		
CFR	Cost and Freight	Kosten und Fracht
CIF	Cost, Insurance and Freight	Kosten, Versicherung, Fracht
CPT	Carriage Paid To	Frachtfrei
CIP	Carriage and Insurance Paid to	Frachtfrei versichert
Group D		
DAF	Delivered At Frontier	Geliefert Grenze
DES	Delivered Ex Ship	Geliefert ab Schiff
DEQ	Delivered Ex Quay	Geliefert ab Kai
DDU	Delivered Duty Unpaid	Geliefert unverzollt
DDP	Delivered Duty Paid	Geliefert verzollt

Index

Bibliografische Information der Deutschen Nationalbibliothek
Die Deutsche Nationalbibliothek verzeichnet diese Publikation in der Deutschen Nationalbibliografie; detaillierte bibliografische Daten sind im Internet über http://dnb.d-nb.de abrufbar.

ISBN 978-3-648-10148-5
Bestell-Nr. 00341-0001

Redaktionsanschrift: Fraunhoferstraße 5, 82152 Planegg
Fon (0 89) 8 95 17-0, Fax (0 89) 8 95 17-2 50
E-Mail: online@haufe.de
Internet: www.haufe.de
Redaktion: Jürgen Fischer

Konzeption und Realisation: Sylvia Rein, 81371 München
Lektorat: Lesley Engel, 83674 Gaißach
Umschlaggestaltung: Kienle gestaltet, 70178 Stuttgart
Druck: freiburger graphische betriebe, 79108 Freiburg

Die Autoren

Sander Schroevers

ist Berater im Bereich der internationalen Kommunikation sowie Keynote Speaker auf Konferenzen und Seminaren weltweit. Er hat zahlreiche Bücher auf dem Feld der internationalen Kommunikation veröffentlicht (www.schroevers.eu). Daneben ist er Präsident des IECIE-Gremiums (l'institut européen de communication internationale d'entreprise) in Paris. Er unterrichtet Interkulturelles Management an der Amsterdamer Hochschule für Angewandte Wissenschaften im Fachbereich Economics and Management, Studienrichtung International Business and Languages.

Ian R. Lewis

Ian R. Lewis stammt aus Irland und ist als Dozent an der Amsterdamer Hochschule für Angewandte Wissenschaften im Fachbereich Economics and Management tätig. Er unterrichtet internationales Verhandeln, Geschichte, Politik, Kultur europäischer und asiatischer Länder sowie Interkulturelle Studien, Studienrichtung Trade Management Asia. Er verfügt über langjährige Erfahrung im internationalen Handel und auf dem Gebiet internationaler Beziehungen.